THE
LONG SHORE

THE
LONG SHORE

A PSYCHOLOGICAL EXPERIENCE
OF THE WILDERNESS

JANE HOLLISTER WHEELWRIGHT
LYNDA WHEELWRIGHT SCHMIDT

Sierra Club Books ■ *San Francisco*

The Sierra Club, founded in 1892 by John Muir, has devoted itself to the study and protection of the earth's scenic and ecological resources—mountains, wetlands, woodlands, wild shores and rivers, deserts and plains. The publishing program of the Sierra Club offers books to the public as a nonprofit educational service in the hope that they may enlarge the public's understanding of the Club's basic concerns. The point of view expressed in each book, however, does not necessarily represent that of the Club. The Sierra Club has some sixty chapters coast to coast, in Canada, Hawaii, and Alaska. For information about how you may participate in its programs to preserve wilderness and the quality of life, please address inquiries to Sierra Club, 730 Polk Street, San Francisco, CA 94109.

LIBRARY OF CONGRESS CATALOGING-IN-PUBLICATION DATA

Wheelwright, Jane Hollister.
    The long shore : a psychological experience of the wilderness / by Jane Hollister Wheelwright, Lynda Wheelwright Schmidt.
    p. cm.
    ISBN 0-87156-625-7

    1. Nature–Psychological aspects. 2. Environmental psychology. 3. Wheelwright, Jane Hollister. 4. Schmidt, Lynda W. 5. Northwest, Pacific–Biography. I. Schmidt, Lynda W. II. Title.
BF353.5.N37W44 1991
155.9'1—dc20   90-46048
                                                                                        CIP

JACKET DESIGN BY ABIGAIL JOHNSTON
BOOK DESIGN AND COMPOSITION BY PARK PRESS

SIERRA CLUB NATURE AND NATURAL PHILOSOPHY LIBRARY
BARBARA DEAN, SERIES EDITOR

Printed in the United States of America on recycled paper.

10 9 8 7 6 5 4 3 2 1

DEDICATION

*To Jo and Klaus,
with love and appreciation
for your patience
and encouragement.*

ACKNOWLEDGMENTS

With gratitude to our editor, Barbara Dean, who turned a heap of material into a book, and gave us all the moral support we could have asked for.

And thanks to Holly Hyde Heifetz for our title,
The Long Shore.

Contents

INTRODUCTION

~ LYNDA ~

In the spring of 1978, my mother invited me to spend a few days with her on the ranch where we both had grown up. Ten years before, in 1968, the ranch had been sold. About one-third of its thirty-nine thousand acres had been turned into a cooperative agricultural venture, with many small parcel holders. My mother had bought back a parcel and put a house on it. It was to this place she invited me.

It took six and one-half years to complete the arrangements of the ranch sale, and during that time my mother made a massive effort to disengage herself from her strong ties to that vast property and to understand how her childhood experiences there had affected the rest of her life. She photographed the ranch from every angle she could reach on foot or horseback. What she could not reach by these means she photographed from a helicopter. She wrote up the solitary day trips she made on horse and on foot in order to experience it thoroughly one more time before it was lost forever. She pulled herself out of her unconscious identity with the land, sky, and ocean by transforming her raw experiences of them into photographs and the written word. The notes she made are the basis for her narrative in this book.

In spite of her efforts to free herself from the ranch, some deep tie remained.

A few years after it was sold, she and I discussed the offer made to her by the new owners of the property. They were developing what had been known to us as "the coast ranch," or "the home ranch," fourteen thousand acres lying along the Pacific Ocean, into hundred-acre parcels, and they wanted to sell her the parcel of her choice for half price. Should she buy back a piece of the ranch?

As far as I was concerned, the answer was an unequivocal "Yes!" I had made no effort to let the ranch go. Perhaps the fact that my mother had worked so hard on her separation from the place had freed me from having to do so myself. She had always given me copies of the photos she took and kept me informed of the events there. Also, in 1970, soon after the ranch was sold, my husband, Klaus, and I had acquired some acreage in the "gold country" of the Sierra Nevada foothills. It shared a border with the El Dorado National Forest, so I had again a place to be in the wilderness. I realize now that I had transferred much of my ranch attachment to this old placer mining area near Placerville, California.

But when the opportunity arose to secure ourselves anew on the ranch, I felt enormous relief and gladness. I went out with the ranch foreman on horseback to look over the coast ranch, where we had lived for generations. My mother had asked me to choose a parcel for her. The one I liked best is, significantly, Parcel Number One. It is located at the high point of the ranch, about fifteen hundred feet up on a rocky ridge, and spreads across a steep brush and scrub oak–covered slope. It tapers to a point halfway down the canyon to form a triangle. It overlooks Point Conception, the ocean, and, on clear days, the Channel Islands off Santa Barbara. At its foot are soft, round hills characteristic of that canyon country and, below them, the mesas on which hay has been grown ever since I can remember. There is a 180-degree vista from east to west, with a full southern exposure. Hawks and buzzards fly past the windows of the house my parents built on the property. Below the house is a small pool, which provides water for many different animals. Even a mountain lion drinks there.

This book on the wilderness arose out of the relationship my mother and I have developed over the past several years. It was because of the fact that we had grown up on the same wild ranch, in our respective eras, that we were able to discover our communality and the way in which our lives were still being influenced by the wilderness.

I had grown up thinking my mother was irrelevant, while she had been very busy finding out just how relevant she was in ways other than mothering. Both of us had been caught by the attractive aspects of the patriarchy, including the freedom and range of choice permitted to men in choosing how they wanted to live their lives. We did not realize until recently that the price of that attitude was the loss of our essential selves and the satisfying relationship she and I might have had all along. We had both seen that men had more interesting lives, while women were limited to being domestic without a worldly life or professional without a family life. Understandably, my mother chose the apparently more interesting life and became a Jungian analyst. She arranged for a nanny-housekeeper for the daily supervision of my brother's and my childhood. Equally understandably, I, in reaction, chose the opposite, staying home with my children. I was finally forced out into a broader life, however, by the energy inherited from both sides of my family and by the ground swell of the women's movement. I became a Jungian analyst, too.

For both of us, then, the approach to life had been one-sided for years, and the chasm between us was wide, given that we had chosen opposite ways to orient our lives. We did not see that we were each half of the story and that together we could complete the story. Until I became an analyst, we kept our distance from each other, preferring to have no relationship than to fight from opposite sides of a single issue.

This issue of our orientation to life came to light in the late 1960s, when two things happened to activate our long-dormant relationship. One was the sale of the ranch. The other was my mother's offering me a chance to read the first draft of her study of Sally. Sally, at thirty-seven, was just my age at the time. She was dying of cancer when my mother was asked by a mutual friend to become her analyst. The friend felt that the analytical process might ease Sally's suffering by providing a framework for the tragedy that would give it meaning. My mother hoped also that Sally might, through the exploration of the unconscious, have a taste of her life as it might have been, and so be able to die with some sense of completion.

Partly it was the fact of my being Sally's age, but mostly it was the direct and devoted care my mother gave her, that moved me. Suddenly I realized that my mother was much more than a professional woman. She conveyed in that first manuscript the depth of feeling, the fierceness of loyalty, the strength of attention that the animal mother gives her babies. She connected with Sally as fully as she could, working without regard for her own fears of the unknown and death, and in spite of Sally's negativity. She put aside without hesitation her own fatigue from the accelerated intensity and frequency of sessions. She noted, but tolerated calmly, her revulsion at Sally's increasing physical deterioration, and Sally therefore did not have to make an effort to protect my mother's feelings in those last gruesome weeks.

I told my mother at once of the significance to me of her work with Sally, and the relationship between us began to open up. Over the next ten years, we gradually came to know each other, though our world views remained one-sided. Men still seemed to have what was best in life, from our standpoint.

But as my mother and I began really to talk to each other in that spring of 1978, when I stayed with her on the ranch, our standpoint changed. At first we talked about the ranch and our feelings about it. We exchanged stories of our childhoods and our relations to the various areas of the property, of working cattle, of the horses, the family, the cowboys. We found how we were similar and different as ranch children and how our experiences compared and contrasted.

While walking along the beach on another trip I made to the ranch, we discussed papers we were writing. My reactions to her work and hers to mine opened more doors in our recognition of each other.

And so we proceeded in the delicate business of finding how we valued each other. The key to all this was that the context of the ranch gave us a naturalness with each other that meetings in a city setting could not have done. I felt that the ranch was mother to us both, giving us an opportunity to explore our relationship as peers, as siblings, as women together.

Though we had lived in, as well as on, the ranch, we had no

conscious understanding of what that meant to us until we started talking. Gradually, we came to see that the ranch had provided us with the security one usually receives from a human mother. It held us in its embrace, gave us a feeling of belonging, taught us to survive. The ranch had been a container in our childhoods, which had had no supervision.

As my mother and I discussed childhood adventures in our respective eras, I realized another similarity between us. Because she and my father had lived 350 miles away in San Francisco, building their practices as Jungian analysts, I had worked out my childhood security on the ranch as she had done in her own unsupervised childhood there, through pairing off with a mate rather than leaning on her parents. I had duplicated her twinship with her brother, Clinty, in making a special alliance with my cousin Jimmy, who was closest to me in age. I came to understand that my attitude of self-reliance and my seeking of peers was inherited directly from my mother, as she had inherited it from her parents, and as I had passed it on to my children.

In this way of comparing notes, my mother and I realized that in the absence of personal mothering we both had turned to the ranch for mothering. Since discussing this phenomenon with her, I have discovered that this substitution of the mother archetype is what happens when personal mothering is absent. An unmothered child, as both my mother and I were, will tend to turn elsewhere—to another adult, to peers, to animals, to a place—for his or her security. "Archetype" refers to a suprahuman representation of human experience, an impersonal and collective symbol of meaning. The archetype of the mother can be experienced in many ways, through a school, a neighborhood, a pet, an organization. In dreams the mother archetype can appear as a whale, an elephant, a bear. We all know nature as "Mother Nature," and the ocean has been called "The Mother of Us All." The particular archetype discovered by any individual depends on his or her own circumstances.

For my mother and me, the ranch provided the "maternal" centering and guidance we needed. When we discovered that the ranch had been mother to us both, we found a bond that has been developing ever since. Sharing our memories and comparing our reactions to similar experiences has made us aware of a connection that neither of us had any idea of for the first half of my life.

What follows in these chapters has to do with my mother's and my experiences of ourselves and the wilderness. Our experiences of place, people, animals, and events can now be drawn forth. Because we were lucky enough to keep a small piece of that once-wild ranch, we have been able to gain a larger sense of the wilderness.

From our present vantage point, we can see how we were bound in a symbiotic tie with the ranch. We can see, now, how we had to break free of that bond, though we felt a great loss in doing so. We both sought a perspective on ourselves and our lives that for us could be found only in consciousness, which in turn required the "unnatural" life of the city. Though we hated leaving our "natural" setting, we both knew instinctively that we had to do so in order to feel complete. Losing everything, we not only gained ourselves in a new way but also came to understand the value of our ranch life for the first time. Even as one has to leave one's mother, so did we have to leave the ranch, in order to come back to it in a new, freer way.

Perhaps it has taken loss after loss of wilderness territories, with the constant threat of losing it all, to give us all a chance to discover its value.

And just what is its value? From our explorations of the meaning of the ranch wilderness in our lives, we formulated larger questions about the need for, and meaning of, the wilderness in contemporary life. The subject is especially poignant now because we are rapidly losing that wilderness. Do we know just what it is that we are losing?

We citizens of the United States are a paradoxical people. We came to America because it was wild and undeveloped. Here we could expand our lives, unrestrained by the class, custom, and ritual of our previous cultures. Yet, over the past 350 years, we have systematically reduced the wilderness and encouraged development along the very same lines that so constrained us in our countries of origin.

Presumably we had no choice. People need some custom and ritual, if not class lines. If it is true that ontogeny recapitulates phylogeny (that the development of the individual repeats the development of the species), *Homo sapiens* will tend to repeat in a new place the same development it has always made over recorded history. Hunting and gathering first, then agriculture, then cities. And that is what has happened in America.

Always we have pushed on. First we pushed across the continent. Then we pushed development—in cities, transportation, industry. Then we sought frontiers in space and ocean. Always forward looking. Those who came to America were the particularly restless ones—explorers, innovators, developers—and the attitude still prevails. "What's new?" we say.

As my mother and I pool our thoughts here, we must look backward. Nostalgia has become another product. Beneath this opportunism, there is a true yearning, I feel sure, and our memories of the wilderness reflect that yearning.

It used to be that America was a number of towns and cities surrounded by wilderness. Now we have patches of wilderness surrounded by civilization. It feels to me as though the tail is beginning to wag the dog.

There is a certain inevitability about all this, since we seem determined to multiply as a species. Only China has taken a stand on reproduction, encouraging its people to have no more than one child or else endure great censure. The strain on the Chinese is enormous, judging from the negative results of this edict, and there is great difficulty in getting people to accommodate to this restriction.

I cannot imagine Americans ever consenting to such limitation on their freedom. It is not only in America that having children is seen as good, either. Even with problems of overpopulation it is hard to imagine anyone saying that it is more important to have wilderness than babies. Yet we may be coming to that choice.

I hope that we can uncover and bring to light the meaning the wilderness carries for everyone. And the fact that we may lose the wilderness may be the necessary trigger for our coming to know its value—as my mother and I came to know the value of our wilderness when we lost it.

Luckily, some of our wilderness areas are hard to develop. Driving across Nevada, or the Rockies, or Texas, as I did recently, confirms that for me. So we probably still have time in those areas. But our forests and grasslands have shrunk and will continue to shrink. We have no time left there. We are losing them, as surely as my family was losing the ranch during the six and one-half years it took to negotiate the sale.

Now that we Americans have enough of a history to call to us, we will, perhaps, look backward as much as we do forward. We are suspended in time between past and future; looking back may enhance the forward view. Looking back, we see the wilderness as it was and can apply our conscious thought to it as we could not when we were struggling for life within it. Looking backward permits an objectivity impossible to the present or future. Objectivity permits evaluation. We are in a position now to discover just how the wilderness is valuable to us. I believe you *can* go home again via consciousness. The wilderness is no longer taken for granted, and it is, in an important sense, home.

In the pages that follow, my mother takes us through the seasons of the ranch, exploring the look, feel, and meaning of the place and the understanding she now has of its value. Through her stories will run the themes of loss and separation as she accepts the sale of the ranch. In accepting that loss, she has come to understand that we must not accept the loss of our planet's wilderness; she develops her understanding of the meaning to us all of wild places and wildlife as she proceeds through the story of our ranch. To illustrate her ideas about our relation to our planet, she relies on the extensive journal notes she recorded during the process of liquidating the ranch.

I will intersperse my associations to her narrative, based on my own experiences as a child there and expanding on the themes suggested above.

THE
LONG SHORE

1

HISTORY OF THE RANCH

~ LYNDA ~

We lived on the ranch one hundred years; I was of the fourth generation. My daughters had some contact with it, too, but the ranch did not become a reference source for them as it did for all of us who came before them.

In 1851, my great-grandfather, William Welles Hollister, rode out to California from Ohio to see what all the gold rush excitement was about, and realized at once that the best possibility for making a fortune was not in the digging of gold but in the feeding and clothing of miners. He saw scarcity and high prices in both meat and wool, and so, the next year, he left Ohio with a flock of six thousand well-bred merino sheep. It took him nine months to make the crossing, and by then most of his flock was gone—dead or stolen or abandoned because of hopelessly ruined hooves. But with the two thousand or so remaining sheep and lambs, he established a ranch in Monterey County, California. In the next ten years, he built up a flourishing business in meat and wool, sold out, moved to what is now Lompoc in Santa Barbara County and set himself up again, and again sold out and moved near the town of Santa

Barbara. Together with two friends, Albert and Thomas Dibblee, he gathered together more than a hundred thousand acres of land, most of it acquired very cheaply.

The partnership eventually broke up, and Great-grandfather's share amounted to approximately thirty-nine thousand acres of undeveloped California property, including eighteen thousand acres on the coast with twenty miles of beaches, plus three smaller ranches inland and another small coastal piece.

Great-grandfather died in 1886, Great-grandmother in 1908; so their youngest living son, John James Hollister, called Jim, took over the management of the ranches. In 1910, Grandfather moved his wife and four children—of whom the only daughter was my mother—onto the largest property, the coast ranch.

My mother lived on the ranch from the time she was four or five until she left to be married in 1929, except when she was away at school. My mother and my father, Joseph, both studied abroad with the Swiss psychologist Carl Jung and ultimately became Jungian analysts, living in San Francisco. While establishing themselves in practice, they arranged for my brother, John, and me to live with Grandmother and Grandfather Hollister on the ranch. I was seven and John was four.

The ranch carries a central meaning for both of us, as it does for my mother and did for her father, partly because we came to it so young and partly because of the place itself.

The main, or coast, ranch, called the Santa Anita after a canyon at its midpoint, lay on the only coastal strip of California that runs east-west. Originally it extended to Refugio Canyon, more than twenty-five miles east of Point Conception, its other end point, and was called *La Nuestra Señora del Refugio*. As part of the only Spanish land grant in the area—the others being Mexican and more recent—the Santa Anita had historical meaning that is rare in California. The land was deeded to Captain José Francisco Ortega in recognition of his services as sergeant on the Portolá expedition, which discovered San Francisco Bay. The reversal of fortunes suffered later by the Spanish in that area was evidenced by the fact that there was a cowboy on the ranch named

Billy Ortega when I was "cowboying" as a young girl. I remember him as an enthusiastic young man of good humor, prepared to take on the most problematical horse or assignment. But he owned no land.

Captain Ortega sold the ranch to the Carrillos, who sold it to the Lobreros, who sold it in 1868 to my great-grandfather.

Every canyon on the ranch had been given a Spanish name, undoubtedly because in the early days the Mexican vaqueros had to know specifically where they were to go to do their assignments. Names were thought up in a hurry; there was no time to let them evolve.

The westernmost canyon, at Point Conception, was called El Cojo, meaning "the lame man." It had been named by Portolá's men for the chief of Shisholop, a Chumash Indian village there. Two others, San Augustine and Santa Anita, were named after saints. Gato (cat) and Coyote were named for animals; Bulito, for "drinking horn" (originally called Las Bolitas, for "mushrooms"); Sacate for "range grass"; Gaviota for "sea gull"; and Agua Caliente for "hot springs," which no longer rose in that canyon even when my mother was a child. The hot springs had been shifted, apparently by an earthquake, to Gaviota Canyon, farther to the east.

In all, there were about twenty canyons. I remember that when I was seven and newly arrived on the ranch, I scrambled to learn their names as fast as possible as part of my effort to work my way into acceptability on the ranch.

Portola's diary mentions three Chumash Indian villages on what became our coast ranch: Shisholop at El Cojo, Catch Tayet at the Santa Anita, and Onomio at the Gaviota. Apparently about two hundred Chumash had thrived on the land that in my mother's day supported only her immediate family. Chiseled chert spears and arrowheads surfaced on the steep banks along the shore and on canyon trails. On the mesas and flats we found steatite bowls and pestles, materials for which must have been quarried by the Indians on the Santa Barbara Channel island called San Nicolas. One bowl more than two feet in diameter was ploughed up from the field that lay between the Big House (my grandparents' house) and the ocean.

This stretch of coast had been thickly populated the year round by the Chumash because of the rich supply of ocean fish. The extensive offshore kelp beds fed a vast chain of sea life, as they do off the coasts of Peru and northern Chile, where large aboriginal maritime coastal populations also once thrived.

I remember the old cowboy Dan Gavarra, whom my mother credits with teaching her to ride when she was a child. She identifies him as more Indian than Mexican because of his ash-dark complexion and stolid, silent manner, and because of the fact that he was on the job well into his eighties.

~ JANE ~

Point Conception, the west end of our coast ranch, is the most dramatic coastal landmark in California. This is where the coast makes a right-angle turn from the east-west direction to the north and the marine life and water and wind currents change radically. On October 18, 1542, the point had been named *Capa Galera* by the Portuguese Juan Rodríguez Cabrillo, who was reminded of the prow of a galley as he sailed by. It was dubbed *Concepción* by Sebastián Vizcaíno, who unimaginatively renamed most of the coast with the help of his religious calendar. I prefer *Galera* because it describes how the point looks from the sea. (Still more realistically, it resembles a huge animal's snout.) But the word "conception" became a crucial symbol in my life. The ranch, because of its wild isolation, was indeed always the beginning of things for me. And to this day, my creative energy is loosed the moment I set foot there.

La Nuestra Señora del Refugio, or the Santa Anita, as we called it, had the Pacific Ocean as its southern boundary. The Santa Ynez Mountain spur, an impassable wall of chaparral with boulders as big as houses, bordered it on the north. This mountain range, extending in an easterly direction from Point Conception down the California coast, is interrupted only once, by Gaviota Pass. Our ranch was comfortably nestled in between the ocean and the Santa Ynez range. Huge, dark green, ancient oaks filled the canyons. The hills and ridges that divided the canyons were tawny gold in summer, and in winter they were emerald green. Because few of the outlying family cared to traverse the dusty, precarious road, my father had a free hand with the ranch. When the rains came, the road, called The Little Burma Road by the Coast Guard during World War II, was impassable much of the time.

The Southern Pacific Railroad traversed the length of the ranch on its way from San Francisco to Los Angeles. My grandfather's farsightedness and money and ambition for development helped launch it, but it became operable only after he died. In 1900, my father brought his bride to the ranch in the work train's caboose, making them the first passengers to travel the Southern Pacific line. There were no roads or phone or means of travel other than railroad, horseback, or foot. In exchange for the right of way, the train would stop for us at one of three whistle-stops. However, the train could be half a day late, and then we were forced to wait beside the siding for the moment when it would appear, with only a brief warning from a semaphore close by. Because of the rough terrain, the train could not be seen until it was practically upon us. Then someone had to wave a flag, standing on the far rail, until the engineer tooted twice his recognition. With creaking and clanking and streams of steam, the locomotive would bring its train to halt for us to board.

The ranch's gentle, balmy climate was continually freshened by sea air coming off the ocean at Point Conception. The air streamed behind our northern barrier, the mountain ridge, picking up force as it funneled through openings in the wall and down the canyons. As the fresh air flowed around and over obstacles in the rough terrain, it left many pockets of silence in which one could luxuriate. It was never hard to find a cozy, small shelter against the wind.

On Grandfather's death in 1886 my grandmother, who inherited the five ranches, along with heavy debts from the family's extravagances, immediately put them up for sale. She was a city product, having grown up in San Francisco, and the isolation of the ranch had never appealed to her. My father, however, stepped in and reversed his mother's plans. The grass in Santa Anita Canyon, tall enough to tie across his saddle, changed his mind. He said that land that produced grass like that would make a good living for someone. The debts could be paid off, given time.

Astronomical sums had to be borrowed. I remember them as a child and to my distress, because my mother never let any of us forget we were in debt. My parents toiled and struggled and worried until many years later the ranches emerged financially free and clear. For my father, the struggle was a personal one. To pull the ranches through was to pull himself through. The enormous effort cinched his tie to the place.

All in all, it was, however, a miracle that so much land belonged to one family for more than one hundred years in California. That was accomplished in part by factors not of our making. For instance, a large deposit of diatomaceous earth, the fossil remains of billions of microscopic diatoms, was left to my grandfather by his partners, who did not know its value. The local Indians had used the white pigment for rock paintings; in my father's time, it was discovered to be ideal material for filtering and fireproofing and myriads of other uses. These deposits brought in substantial rentals and royalties. There were also exploratory oil leases that paid handsomely during most of my life on the ranch. For these reasons, partly, the ranches had not slipped out of the family possession long ago. When my father was in charge, he saw to it that the windfall money did not go for luxuries. It was instead ploughed back into preserving the land. By World War II, the ranch was on fairly solid financial footing.

After World War II, however, land values began to increase faster than cattle prices. Therefore, taxes and modernization required reinvesting the small profits from the cattle, plus profits from rentals in Santa Barbara and the mineral deposits. Droughts were costly, since they forced us to sell cattle or move them at high cost to other parts of the country with more feed.

And finally, there was loss of cattle quality, since no new blood was coming into the herd. Father insisted on breeding only his original cows and bulls because they were free of anaplasmosis. Once, my twin, Clint, and I bought some new young bulls. Every one of them curled up his toes and died. After that, Clint worked with the University of California at Davis to try to improve the herd, but it was too little, too late. When my father died in 1961, we began the liquidation struggle.

2

THE SECOND GENERATION

~ JANE ~

My father died suddenly. He was ninety-one at the time, and his death put the finishing touches to a long, graceful life. He died as he had lived, stoically, after only three days of severe illness. His going drew to a close the symbiotic, charmed relation between landlord and land that had prospered on the West Coast as far back as the occupation of the Spanish, and of the Chumash Indians for thousands of years before the Spanish arrived. Those following would manage by phone or Jeep or from city-based headquarters.

On Sunday Father was driven over his thirty-nine thousand acres by the ranch superintendent. After an enjoyable lunch at Andersen's in Buellton, he was driven back to his new home in Santa Barbara for supper and his lifetime routine of early bedtime. The following morning something was wrong. He had a violent stomach upset that worried him—more for its threat to his dignity than for the pain.

Two days later he was desperately ill. In the late afternoon, without warning, he rose from the pillow to brace himself on his elbows. "I'm done in," he said, and kissed me. I knew instinctively it was his goodbye.

Later I saw the act as his last gesture of independence and an expression of his nineteenth-century gallantry. He was in charge of himself to the end. By Wednesday he was dead.

During his adult life, my father never gave in to excesses or to behavior that could be criticized. All of that had been taken care of in his youth. Sowing wild oats, it was called in his day. As an adult, he could do no wrong. He was always in good taste, always as though on view. In 1956, in his eighties, when he sat by my mother's deathbed for an entire day and night, he did not once loosen his tie, nor did he lie down to rest. He sat stiffly in his chair the length of his vigil until he was finally persuaded she would never regain consciousness.

My father's end slowly revealed a clue to his life. I am reminded of the analogy Anne Lindbergh used when her husband died: the great tree has fallen. You can at last see all of it. Standing, it was always in perspective. No one I ever knew acted so entirely certain of what he was about, nor followed his own path so relentlessly, regardless of those in his way as he did so, nor blamed himself less. His movements reflected the vast, untouched area he watched over. He was predictable as the seasons; it was as if his every movement was directed by the laws that kept all of nature on its track. His acceptance of death was equally without question. But his impact on the family—especially on my mother—was drastic. That was the other side to the work of nature that he was. Living for the sake of his land had been at a cost. He left the rest of us trapped in a hopeless situation.

My father was handsome, though not dashing, as one expects an excellent horseman to be. He always wore plain khakis, with puttees for protection, never using the flashy Spanish chaparejos, sombrero, and silver inlaid gear he owned. His face, bronzed by a lifetime of sun, was made darker by the contrast of his thick white hair. On ranch business in Santa Barbara he wore what he called his "store clothes"—a gray suit, always of the best cut and quality, and a gray felt hat, slightly tipped to convey his natural confidence. He could have been received anywhere. But never once, to my knowledge, was he seen visiting in any house except his sister's—and then only by "royal command." He never patronized a theater, not even to see a movie. Nor did he ever step into an airplane.

However, my father was by no means a prude. His gentle, natural, graceful nature could be spiced periodically with irreverences. Long ago, when I was a very small child, he was replacing a toilet seat in our house. (He was our reluctant plumber and handyman, since we were too isolated to hire repairmen, and he could fix anything. He had practical sense and had been educated as an engineer at the Massachusetts Institute of Technology.) I can see him to this day, in his almost boyish rebellion. There was no escaping the urgency of the job. Slipping the unattached, newly bought toilet seat over his head, he said to himself with a chuckle, "It's my horse collar."

My father never rode his horse "off a walk" if he could help it. This was the habit of a man who had ridden every day of his life, since there had been no other means of transportation until the era of automobiles. He rode his horse as though to do a job; even during the roundups in his older years, he always rode conservatively, no matter what the conditions. Like an Indian, and as silent, he was part of his horse. You noticed the horse before you saw him.

To my knowledge, my father was never thrown from a horse until he was in his late seventies. That was when Nelly, his fat, white, reliable mare, bucked him into a clump of sagebrush. She was frightened, trying to avoid a badger that had scuttled under her to escape into its hole. Without a word, my father pulled himself out of the brush and handed the reins to one of his men, ordering him to "take her away." The decision was typical of him. Once he made a move that involved preserving his dignity, there was no turning back. In the same way, he disposed of people who offended him. They, like his horse, were ushered out of his life without being offered a second chance. But I like to think his disgust with Nelly was in direct proportion to what his skill with horses had been throughout his life.

My father was as much farmer as horseman. He was constantly concerned and plagued by problems of growing crops in a land of unreliable rainfall; I can still see him, during the rainy season, stepping out onto our lawn to scan the skies. "Bad" weather in those days was never a cause for grumbling. To this day, I react negatively when people rave about sunshine if rain is needed.

My mother was a complete contrast to my father. She was tiny and frail. In her youth she weighed less than a hundred pounds, and even I, later, less than five feet, two inches tall, could look down on her as she tottered around precariously in size four shoes. Mother's hair was golden, abundant, and long enough to sit on; my father never let her forget how beautiful it was, and his admiration kept her from cutting it to suit the fashion. She had bright blue, lively eyes; not a handsome face, but animated. She could laugh until she cried and talked at every opportunity. Her mind was formidable. Too bad if you got in its way! Coming from Sacramento and brought up in the former governor's mansion, she never entered into ranch activities other than to apply her brilliant mind to its paperwork problems. Economics, politics, geology, background studies of all sorts were her interests. My father made no final decision without consulting her.

Father and Mother's courtship was as unlikely as they were a pair. They met in the pioneer class of Stanford University and were engaged for four years after graduation. During that time he prospected for gold in Alaska and she earned a Ph.D. in psychology in Göttingen, Germany, despite knowing no German when she went abroad. From the time they were married in 1900 to the end of her eighty-six years she was only at times a willing captive of the ranch; at others, she was more like a caged wild thing beating at the cage bars. My father chose to ignore her spells of frantic claustrophobia. When I suggested he at least take her to a movie he would say, "Oh, Dot's all right."

My father saw his wealth in terms of numbers of acres and numbers of cattle, never in dollars. He had a peasant's good sense. In regard to the land, his instincts were intact and served his descendants well in the end. But, like his father before him, he put his herds and land before his family.

The land, incorporated into a family business, should have been the concern of all of us. But my father controlled the majority of shares in the family corporation and used his control to keep the vast empire intact to his death. Suggesting that some of it should be disposed of was to suggest disposing of parts of him. He was the land and the land was in him. There was no room for anyone else!

My father maneuvered secretly—and he acted while the rest of us talked. He conformed to management regulations just enough to put off questioning. He would listen attentively to suggestions for modernizing and then quietly, surreptitiously, fall back into his old ways. He knew best; or something in him knew best—and often he was right. He would at times justify his behavior with arguments firmed up through the years, but he never offered explanations until he was pushed to defend his actions.

Unlike my contemporaries in the family, I shared with my father the pleasures of seeing vast herds spread over endless ranges, feeling with him a sense of our land-rich heritage. But only as long as I shared his pride was I accepted into his private world. He lived first for his ranches, second for his wife, third for himself, and not at all for us. His own father had been patriarch to his community but never a father role model to his family. It was not surprising that his sons and nephews felt orphaned. Unable to articulate their hurt, they never understood the feelings behind what was happening. They protested instead with irrational, outspoken hatred and indiscriminate, undifferentiated, de-structive anger. While he remained firm in his feelings of being right, they were, in a way, expressing the other side of him that never showed. For the last ten years of Father's life, his sons and nephews tried to liquidate the company to get their money, but they could not dislodge him. They took him to court for mismanagement at the age of ninety and lost.

My father apparently had been aware of the family frustration long before that event, and from time to time he indirectly let us know by way of a story. All through his life it had been his custom to tell stories, and as a child I remember anticipating with excitement the well-worn punch lines. Finally, as he neared ninety, there was only one story left, about an old cattleman who owned one of the Santa Barbara Channel islands. My father described this old man in detail and with relish, apparently meaning to convey what a tough nut he was. My father said that the old cattleman, not too long before he died, told him he would leave no will. "Let the bastards fight for it," he said. Each time my father told the story he would looked around, innocently and slowly, at the faces around him frozen into silence.

Because of its inaccessibility and protective contours, the ranch became a retreat for most of my father's brothers and their friends— except, of course, for my father himself. But ranches as family affairs, under the best conditions, and for the last twenty years of my father's life, no longer belonged to the California economy. The end was in sight; something beyond us was driving us out. My father's stubborn old age seemed to be part of that something.

The land's impact on my three brothers and three cousins and on my descendants was as drastic as it had been on my father. An imprisoning power was in the land. It still is, but we have not been willing prisoners as my father was. I remember the bitterness of his only sister, who cared about city life and society. The ranch had ruined her four brothers, she said. "That ranch!" No human could have exerted as devastating an influence. No individual could exude such sirenic, compelling power as there was out there. Our whole family was proof of that.

The worse the family situation became, the more hardened my father was in his will to hang on. His obtuseness turned my generation's rugged, individualistic style into a kind of nightmare. Rather than driving family members away, the conflict drew them like a magnet to the ranches, as if they wanted to "get in on the kill." The unfocused aggression of the third generation exuded like poison. We became desperate.

3

THE THIRD GENERATION

~ JANE ~

In my generation we were seven: three brothers, three male cousins, and me. Land was our mark of distinction, and we could feel a certain kind of undeserved importance because of it. We all had been so very privileged.

During my father's last years, when he was too frail, really, to manage the family corporation, I had to be his eyes and ears and mouthpiece without his knowing. It was a kaleidoscopic kind of role. Trying to find some balance, some temporary agreement, in our unruly family, I had to speculate from the sidelines, without letting him realize it, on possible ways of selling out. From the start there had been a faction who most resented his adamant rule and wanted "out."

After my father's death, I was unexpectedly left the key person to solve the problem of the disposition of our ranches. I could blame no one. I had, in 1956, created a voting trust, with my father as trustee, to try to save the ranches from damage due to family conflict. He had then designated me successor trustee, which would put me in control of the majority of shares after he was gone. Not his sons and nephews, but I, would take his place! He must have known I was stubborn, like him, and would tackle the insoluble problems. Also, being the only woman in my generation, I was not, like the men, in competition. But the outrage caused by his having chosen me only compounded the already existing confusion.

The family politics were bad enough, but my father's death also unexpectedly let loose in all of us a jumble of inchoate, apparently undigested personal feelings. So the struggle among the seven of us began, lasting until the ranches were sold six and one-half years later.

Walking or riding over our properties month after month during those years of settlement, I tried to understand why their pull was so strong—why I was loath to give up the ranch and why at the same time it felt like a heavy burden. Mostly it had to do with losing virgin land before understanding what it meant to me. I had no guidelines for interpreting its meaning at that time. Father's silence, his disregard of his responsibility for us when we were children, his total identification with the land, his habit of explaining nothing, kept us in a binding ignorance. The Chumash, who might have helped, were gone, their rituals and legends gone with them. The Spanish first, then the Yankees, had brought with them their own ideals based on profits, flower gardens, and houses. These cultural biases, evolved out of foreign lands, allowed them to disregard the advanced culture of the native populations, ignore the beauties of the indigenous vegetation and its food value for stock, and destroy the ecological balance of the area by decimating the wildlife. But I felt I would be lost if I lost this land. Owning this land had been a love affair, which was about to be terminated by circumstances beyond our control. On top of all that, I felt that the special spirit of the place—one we might have known, given more time—had finally turned its back on us; that it was deliberately, vengefully, snubbing us, leaving us in limbo.

But all the time in the background loomed the debatable question: Can the land belong to anyone, or does one belong to the land? My twin brother loved the land in a personal way as much as, if not more than, anyone, but did not know it. My second brother had also, but he had died before its disposal became an issue. My oldest brother and three cousins remained alienated. I was left needing to get at least some inkling of what it was all about. It seemed important that someone understand why love of the land can transcend human love, as it had for my grandfather and my father. And why others of my generation who turned against our heritage were just as caught.

Land is many times more binding than a parent, although its binding effect occurs in something of the same pattern. It is hard enough to have to discover a parental tie, but far more so to uncover the parental significance in so large a piece of land. I was faced with having to recapture, or pull up for the first time, a sense of the land's significance—in my language, to coax back its spirit, if possible. Finding something in the way of meaning to make my own, however, had to be done without the help of dialogue, except insofar as it might be with myself, in the form of notes. I had a strong sense of being buried deep in the soil, lost under the vast, rocky ledges, melted into the landscape, submerged as an integral part of that place. None of the others in my generation had the remotest sense of being so influenced. I was starting at scratch and I felt like a child about to be orphaned.

My own mother's preoccupation with her survival in isolation had made her unavailable to me in my childhood. Being an "outsider," with more objectivity, she might have been able to help; a child's objectivity normally evolves out of the protective understanding of the parent. My objectivity, on the other hand, would have to come directly out of an understanding experience of the immense power of the place itself. My brothers and cousins would have thought this was nonsense had they known these thoughts.

Mulling over the situation, I thought it best to note down faithfully my observations: every small nuance of feeling, all my reflections, memories, and thoughts during the days of exposure to our place. Being free, finally, to go my own way, now that my father was gone, and because there would be some time before the ranches were sold, I undertook to find a thread in all this jumble.

So I was presented with a double dilemma: one, to try to work out a satisfying economic solution to the ranch's financial problems, and two, to try to discover the meaning to me of this great, wild ranch.

Liquidation ultimately would settle both dilemmas, though there would be a high emotional cost. Since cattle could not pay anymore—the costs of running the ranch were just too high—and the family could not tolerate the conflicts of attitude caused by lifelong dissatisfactions, selling out would prove to be the only solution.

~ LYNDA ~

In thinking about what my mother has said up to this point, I am reminded of how it felt to have no dog for the first time in my life. Because of major life changes, my husband and I could not get a new dog for several years after our old dog died in 1982. In a very small way, living without a dog was like living without the ranch, a combination of sadness and relief.

I remember the deep emptiness when the ranch was sold, the flat sorrow, the feeling of being bereft. I felt stripped; there was no buffer between me and the outer world of civilization and society. I had no sense of place.

At the same time, I remember the relief I felt that the family conflict was over at last. I had grown up with the conflict, feeling it long before I even knew what the word meant. As a child, I would listen to conversations between my grandparents as they discussed the behavior and comments of my uncles, my mother's brothers. Always it seemed as if my uncles were wrong and causing trouble. Then, in my uncles' homes, the discussions would take the opposite view, and my grandparents seemed to be wrong and causing needless trouble. My mother had had little to say about any of these things until she herself got involved in the ranch again, in the 1950s. And then she got caught up in the conflict too.

I lived with her father and mother, my grandparents, from age seven to ten, and then every summer for three months after that until they became too old, after which I spent summers with one of my uncles' families. From my child's view, Grandfather was as my mother describes him. Without talking, except when he had to, he ruled the ranch absolutely. A graphic example of this was his plunging all the houses in the home canyon into darkness every night at nine o'clock. He had a long length of rope attached to the "off" switch on the generator from which we all derived our electricity. At nine o'clock he would give the rope a great yank and shut down the generator. In explanation, he said he wanted everyone to go to sleep early in order to get up early. And, indeed, he was on the phone at seven in the morning to be sure everyone was on his way to work.

We had butane, too, as an auxiliary energy source, so I would read after the electricity was shut off. But from their room next to mine, my grandparents could see my light under their door. Within fifteen minutes or so, Grandmother would call out, "Now you turn off that light, d'you hear?" in a tone that permitted no argument. So I would turn it off. It was inconceivable that I argue with either of them about anything. Mostly I went my own way and saw relatively little of them. If I needed to get up in the night I used my flashlight, if it had not rolled away somewhere in the big three-quarter-size bed I slept in.

Later, as a teenager, I did go out sometimes with Grandfather in his blue Jeep to inspect the properties and the men's activities. He was in his late seventies by then, and no longer rode out on horseback. The trips in the Jeep were typical of him; he seemed willing enough that I be there, but he clearly wanted no conversation.

When we came up to one or more of the crew, working on the fence line or training a young horse or haying, he would get out of the Jeep, greet the men briefly, look around and say a word or two more, and climb back in the Jeep, and we would drive off.

I know, from my years of "cowboying" on the ranch, going on roundups and doing corral work afterward, that the men utterly respected Grandfather. They referred to him as "the Old Man," and they rarely let us grandchildren hear anything negative about him.

But it must have been very difficult to be his child. My mother always conveyed to me her admiration of him, even when as an old man he would block her efforts to make the ranch pay or just stubbornly stand pat in the face of modern agricultural methods. But he must have been too remote and silent to be a good father to her and her three brothers. She tells the story of getting a rare letter from him when she was away at school. It was mimeographed and began with the salutation "Dear Son."

I can see how the issue of the disposition of the ranches would have brought to the surface all the frustration in the three sons and their three cousins. Although the discussions centered on practical issues of finances, taxes, the decline of big cattle ranches in California, and the enormous value of undeveloped coastal property for other purposes, the true subject must have been, at least partly, the issue of grown men chafing under an autocratic, very long lived father. He was a figure from the past: an impressive, confident, distant ruler of his domain. And the Western world of the 1960s no longer accepted such authority. New values were appearing, and preserving a vast, wild private property was not one of them.

So, as a child, silently moving through the various family houses, I knew that something was always wrong. And later, when my mother was left with the power of voting the majority of the stock, I saw the conflict rise to a great pitch. As the only woman in her generation of seven, and from the resultant bond between father and daughter, she had a special link to the past, to her father's world. Through this positive connection with her father, which the others did not have, she felt the legacy of the history of the place and his identification with it; selling it would be like selling him out, as well as signing the death warrant of a beautiful entity. And, from my view, it was partly because of their resentment at Grandfather's autocratic attitude and a need for redress for their years of frustration that her cousins and oldest brother wanted to sell. (My mother's twin, Clinty, was not for selling, and her middle brother, Joe, had died by then.)

Whatever the reasons for the conflict, I saw my mother gradually yield: not only to the force of the men's arguments but also to the sad reality of social change. It was no longer possible to preserve a private property of such size by running cattle on it. The profits were barely enough to pay the ever-rising property taxes. There was virtually no income from the company stock. The ranch was becoming an indulgence. Its doom was inevitable.

My mother began her effort to free herself from the ranch by coming to know how attached to it she was.

4

THE MESAS

~ JANE ~

From my present vantage point, in my eighties, I read my notes from more than twenty-five years ago with a knowledge of what was then my unconscious identity with nature's grand scheme. Now, scientists are reporting their religious sense of awe of nature, but then, because of the bias of those times, I felt that being part of nature meant that I was perhaps only sinking regressively into the primitive past. Now, scientists are sounding their alarms for our planet, but then, the word "progress" usurped the front page. I realize now that I have been no better than my fellow beings who still believe that where there is a will there is a way, since I, too, am part of the modern technological world. But at the same time, my notes show me that all my life, without knowing it, I have been siding with the gods of the Indians through my love and respect for every living wild thing. In my encounter with the mesas in January 1962, messages from the land itself, emerging in what I wrote then, were telling me that here was my living home and my real parent, even my excuse for living.

My notes from January 1962 also describe the continuation of family turmoil triggered by the ever-present threat of loss of our properties. The clamor to sell was always there, especially on the first Tuesday of every month, when our company's board of directors met. Before and after those Tuesdays, however, I could roam over the ranches to my heart's content, safely out of reach of this backdrop of human struggle. Ironically, it was because of these meetings that I could experience the coast ranch in its many moods. With its peace and quiet I could also clear my thoughts a little about its future.

My sadness at the growing threat to sell must have been showing, because I was constantly being told, "You can't make a living by ranching as a way of life." This was also the phrase used by the experts at the agricultural college, the University of California at Davis, to differentiate between ranching as a business and ranching as a hobby. My feelings for the land were being called "sentimental," sometimes with a sneer, because, as we all knew, we could not afford so big a ranch as a hobby. Yet, sentimental or not, the sadness persisted.

Early in the month, I drove to the western end of the coast ranch and for the first time took in deliberately part of the country I had known intimately for many years. With my senses heightened, if not aggravated, by the mounting family pressures, I looked at what was before me as though I had never seen it before.

Once out of the car at the end of the road, I was assaulted by the beauty of the place. Why should this place, just now, be so beautiful? Why now! Was it because of impending loss? Why? I became indignant: beauty cannot flaunt itself to the horizons so irresponsibly! Or, if it can, beauty must be forced to give up its message and let loose its grip. Or— it must be preserved at all cost. These thoughts unleashed a burst of energy such as I had never felt before. They focused me onto every vista, every nuance, every living thing, animate or inanimate, around me. Flooded by impressions, I noted down every detail I was looking at in the notebook I had adopted as my constant companion six months earlier.

Why should a place we no longer could afford—a place that was destroying what was left of an old pioneer family—hold us enthralled in hate? Could its power be the beauty stretched out before me: the white light that flooded everything and the new green in the oaks that browned to an earth tone with a little yellow in it? Or the dark, energetic green of the aggressive, defiant grass, not tall but toughened by generations of droughts to thrive in places where the soil is deep? Long-verdant blades, that day bending over with their own weight, caught the sun where they bent. Because of the rainy season, the gray-green of the sage had lost its dusty pallor; it no longer had the look of death. All this burst of green, set off by the bright white light, reflected to a blinding intensity. The words tumbled out like wild things caged and at last set free.

Compulsively, I continued to look around. Impressions, unknow-ingly and indelibly laid down a million times over, like thin layers of silt carried in the flow of years living there, revealed themselves for the first time. I wondered: There had to be more to the power of the land than was held in the colors and contours. The problem must go deeper.

On land, everything was radiant. Out to sea, a stillness and a waiting mood prevailed, with clouds coming reluctantly out of the southeast. The ocean was dove gray and smooth as velvet, with no sharp line at all on the horizon. Out there it all melted together—the water, the sky, the clouds—except for a single ship's wake, which had somehow caught a stray bit of sun that escaped through a concealed opening in the clouds.

How can one live one's youth in such a place and not notice its fatal attraction until all of a sudden, when loss is imminent and the whole phenomenon bursts into a kind of tidal-wave need for recognition? The word "fatal" expressed my feelings exactly. It seemed to me that this land must have ruthlessly cut into those of us (my twin and me, certainly) who were reared on it from a very early age. Its tyrannical power, its unknown mystery, must have drawn us all down to a level known only to the aborigines, which we could not articulate. These instinctive, sacred, magical territorial rights that may have trapped all of us were essential to wild life; but certainly they were not part of enlightened humanity? Or—wait a minute; maybe they were. How else to explain so powerful a pull? Or was this attraction the key to the origin of the human self-center, without which man is only a rootless poor thing? Was I discovering that our great Earth Mother, concentrated as a total force in every small plot as well as in every great estate, had bound us with an umbilical cord without our knowledge? Was "She," then, our self-center, and were we only pawns in a larger scheme that made our coast special for us?

So strong were my feelings of being caught in some fateful determination that I was tempted to conclude that the white, the green, the soft, flowing contours—that perfection—had come down on us (on the unthinking and thinking alike) with a viselike, destructive grip, spelling out for every one of us a kind of doom. We, as individuals, just might be nothing apart from this living, breathing vastness. The thought was frightening. The devil himself was ensconced in paradise.

Looking away from the sea and toward the hills, I could see on their steep northern slopes a green made lighter by a slight yellow cast in it. The cooler sun rays weaken the grass there. Any yellow is a pleasing accompaniment to the gray of the sage.

The clean harrow marks on the rising contours of the mesa were perfect, repeated in a spreading, fanlike way to infinity. Here and there the small mud basins, formed by the hardpan of the road, proved there had been half an inch of rain three or four days earlier. Where the cattle had been sloshing to their hocks in mud, their hoof marks were caked solid by the sun: faithful plaster casts, inverted but exactly fitting the cloven hooves. A bright green oak, slightly browned by overripe oak flowers hanging in short, fat tassels, stood against the soft sky. The broad, fine earthen gray of the planted slope led up to the tree like an apron.

Everything I could see was flawless—infuriatingly opposite to, yet undoubtedly coming out of, my deep-down feelings of defeat. By then the decision to sell was only temporarily being stymied by the few grimly hanging on.

The feelings of defeat and loss were connected; also intermingled were my own pangs of guilt for having gone along with those who wanted to sell, for not having openly resisted them and held on at all cost. I felt a heavy disappointment at the human ruthlessness all around me. Our moral obligation should have been to save our land from industry, for which it had been declared qualified because of the prevailing offshore winds (the pollution from industrial use theoretically would be drained off or blown out to sea). We should also have made an effort to save the land from the mediocrity of a second-home development. Had I decided to fight against the sale, the few who wanted to keep the land at all costs would have supported me against threatened legal action. They would have paid my expenses, they said.

Others gave us friendly advice to sell, knowing that so much family strife meant we could not have developed the ranch to the point where it could be self-supporting. We never could have raised the necessary capital. Our ranch no longer could compete profitably in agriculture because it lacked the amount of water that specialty crops require. The state did not have the funds to make it into a park. But there was always in my ears an impersonal order from "out there" somewhere, as though the land had a voice of its own, to decide against the "friendly" advice. "Don't let it go to the highest bidder," that voice said. With the arguments still echoing in my head, I continued to record what lay around me.

This was always a smiling country in the quiet January season. The coastline mesas were sunny; they gaily basked in the southern exposure. More than twenty miles of dirt road snaked across them, its back broken periodically in this wet season by gullies and washouts. Most people considered the road dangerous; I, on the other hand, felt ensured a delicious privacy.

From where I stood at El Cojo Creek, a sharp, dark background of rough mountains to the east rose as a protective frame to the soft, light green landscape in the many miles of foreground. Barely inland, beyond the rock strata, the Vaqueros Sands, identified years ago by my geologist brother, lay as far as I could see down the coast. The Sands is a long, broad, bare strip of outcropping sandstone that dances rhythmically into the haze, up and over and down each of the many north-south parallel ridges. The ridges, like vertebral columns, connect the many soft, rounded hills overlooking the mesas to the mountain range behind.

The mesas were once the continental shelf and are now, according to some, continuously and imperceptibly, by geological pressures, still moving. Golden tan in the dry summer, in winter the mesas become vistas of glaring green grass. My father had always boasted about our grass-fat cattle, naturally fed by the mesas, before the feedlot era made it necessary to force-feed cattle into grotesque caricatures of themselves.

The alluvial soil of the mesas was molded originally into arbitrary shapes by mysterious movements within ancient ocean depths. The mesas stretch out beyond the huge, rounded, and sometimes conical hill mounds deposited from a still more ancient era—probably a hundred million years ago, when the shoreline was at the Mother Lode. Because of the east-west direction of the California coastline here, these hills face the ocean to the south in an orderly row. It is as though they have only just stepped back off the mesas to straighten their line.

The serenity of the vast, ancient past was still evident. Only a small amount of farming and a few loosely binding fence lines containing the wild cattle had intervened. Contours everywhere, still untampered with by man, vouched for the earth's crust having once been wrenched and tossed by the relentless pressure of moving continents. Evidence of the violence, a great trough in our back country, cut arbitrarily in an east-west direction across the canyons. It had been created by a shale strata called Anita shale, which may still be settling. The Santa Ynez ridge there formed on its northern slope what is known by botanists as a relic area. Varieties of plants long since gone from Southern California because of the San Andreas fault, now growing in the cooler north, still thrived in the relic area. Pygmy oaks, supposedly from the Channel Islands, covered parts of the topmost ridges.

The young mustard, an import from foreign lands, seemed, in its abundance, intent on driving us off the coast. Mustard had, in fact, already reduced our best range drastically below the profit line. The broad-leaved malva commandeered most of what was left of bare places. One could believe there were grasses and clovers there too only by noticing the Mexican steers with their muzzles down and out of sight in the growth.

I was consciously aware for the first time of the silence pressing in on my skin from all sides. But, heavy as the silence was, it was broken into slightly by the small, bell-like sounds of startled birds and by the distant ocean breakers at low tide. I realized, with pleasure, that these very sounds were responsible for the silence. One meadowlark sang without the slightest interference in all that quiet and in all that space. His call-song, a golden declaration of territorial rights, came at first from close by, then from farther away, and again and again from still farther away. His openly announced retreat was orderly. The meadowlark was adding in his own way to the stillness. I thought to myself, How typical of nature to turn away an unwanted newcomer with a weapon of song! Aesthetics were being subordinated to the needs of survival and in their function had become more aesthetic!

I walked across El Cojo Mesa toward the ocean and the railroad tracks, drawn by a magnet into the details of a place that for years had been fixed below the surface of my thoughts. More birds, inconspicuous ones, many little, dark ones, disappeared into thickly scattered brush, whispering. There was so much life in these emaciated sage bushes on the shaled right-of-way. Without warning, a clumsy flicker, his wings on fire, roughed his way out and disappeared down the tracks.

Small lives like these, probably older in history than man, can bind us to our prehistoric past with their unchanged, appropriate forms and uncomplaining, courageous, faithful adherence to the patterns of their existence.

Only perfection could have survived so long: perfection that had been squeezed out of the relentless conditions of existence, which demanded the sacrifice of the sick and deformed. Nothing was wasted; life was persisting with accurate aim and beauty. It was not hard to imagine these birds, tamer than now, scratching for food not far from the short, square, hulking figures of prehistoric man. Of course, his weapons were not so lethal then; and, who knows, he might have found comfort in the gentle creatures, inadvertently sending them down the centuries with a message having to do with the continuity of life.

Our immediate predecessors on this land had had a message, too;

one they could have delivered themselves. They were the Chumash Indians, so named by anthropologists but called *Quabajay* in Portolá's diary. The confusion of names came about through some popular mistakes typical of the early days. The Mi Chumash had originally belonged to Santa Cruz Island, just across the channel from our ranch, but their name, for convenience, now includes all the Indians that lived in an area extending along the coast roughly from San Luis Obispo to Los Angeles: specifically, according to Thomas Blackburn, from Estero Bay to Topanga Canyon and inland to the edge of the San Joaquin Valley. Their area included also the islands of San Miguel, Santa Rosa, and Santa Cruz in the Santa Barbara Channel.

In my childhood the Chumash were burdened with the better-known name "Diggers," which had been given them by pioneers who, on their westward trek, had encountered desert Indians living on roots. The degrading term was to be the prelude to the total extermination of the sophisticated maritime Chumash by the Spanish and Yankees. This extermination was accomplished in less than a hundred and fifty years, from the late 1700s to May 5, 1941, when Juan Justo, one of the last surviving full-blooded Chumash Indians, died. A peaceful and far from barbarous people, possibly numbering six to seven thousand in the Santa Barbara area, was driven to disease and death by my forebears, descendants from the so-called civilized European continent.

This total disregard of our native predecessors was, I had always felt, a symptom of some disenchantment with some aspect of ourselves, the invaders. Curiously, those of us who put profits before the welfare of the land also felt that discontent. This was part of the message telling me not to sell.

A vague fear rode hard on these thoughts: were we ruthlessly destroying other symbols of the continuity of life that had taken so long to develop? In my grandfather's generation, grizzlies had been shot to extinction or exterminated in bull-and-bear fights for the edification of the public. In my era, the pumas had been hunted down, except for a few stragglers, because they threatened the ranchers' profits.

One no longer found horned toads, those comical, tiny, armored, dragonlike creatures that are vulnerable in a disturbed ecology. I had not seen the jeweled kingfisher in years. And it would be only with the greatest good luck that I might come onto a broad rattlesnake, its bold, still diamond back warm and snug in the sun, camouflaged in the gray dust. In my childhood, I had so often seen this grand creature motionless except for a black tongue darting from its large, square head, its pale, transparent rattles slightly raised for warning, waiting for me to pass! There had been too many casualties in the past generation's quarrel with nature.

As I continued to roam, I wondered also about the occasional individuals from a species apparently lost for good that suddenly reappear, entirely at home and as shiny and taut and whole as ever. I remembered, for instance, riding through a forest of ancient oaks the year before in El Cojo Canyon, half a mile from where I stood. The leaf canopy over my head had been festooned with what looked like orange and yellow and black and red and white fruit. I was looking at sapsuckers, which had not been seen in our area for years, relishing the bumper crop of acorns. Those birds had the air of having been there all along; they were complete with their full set of complicated reflexes. Each individual was a symbol of the tenacity of life, yet they did not appear at all like wild things struggling back to reestablish themselves in the face of encroaching civilization.

In the past, we had taken for granted that in time there would be the return of species that had left our area because of drought, flood, or fire. But no longer. I doubted, for instance, that an oriole would ever come back to build its ingenious suspended woven nest in the jacaranda next to my mother's house. Apparently we can exterminate creatures, but at least we cannot modify them.

Another doomed local wild inhabitant was the condor. He was a grand bird with an incredible blunt scavenging head and a ten-foot span of wings. His shoulders were shining black and heavy and swelling, muscled for flying across the country, circling eighty to a hundred miles in a day. Long white triangles showed under his night-black wings as he slipped into the airstream overhead.

I was not yet in my teens when I first saw these great birds, too many to count, settled on the ground not far from our home. They had come to scavenge. Their overlapping black, broad wings, the primaries fanned out widely, formed a canopy that put out the sun when they rose. The birds turned their heads this way and that in curiosity. Strange and immediate and eerie and unearthly, they were part of the deepest past, of roots that I had long ago adopted without knowing. Now they are only a fading link in the overall life stream.

The memory of them intensified the eroding sense of loss permeating me that day. Even this childhood experience had been an uncanny dip into a former lonelier, grander, wilder, perhaps more barren, era; a reminder of a time of ancient silence and wild space and private sweeps for sensitive creatures. The great birds, which had once scanned the whole continent, protected by enormous, empty skies, were now virtually lost because of their almost total lack of self-protection, the severe reduction of their habitat, and their casual way of reproduction. In their enviable but fatal disregard for time, they hatched one chick every other year; if it survived, it would not fly for ten months and still would not be fully mature for five or six years. Originally that had been fitting for creatures living as long as we do.

There were no condors remaining in the San Rafael Mountains, inland from our land. My childhood encounter with their compelling majesty might not have been the privilege I had always taken it for. Was it possible that those who had never been exposed to such grandeur were better off? That day I thought so. At least those others were not burdened with the regrets and feelings that plagued me about how the world might have progressed had our human intelligence functioned in cooperation with nature.

Out to sea, the brown kelp dirtied the water in broad patches; no doubt one of nature's tricks to save us from the monotony of beauty! The waves were not energetic that afternoon; they barely roused themselves. When they fell they did not pound the sand in the way I remembered.

A small red plastic piece of something on the beach looked at first like a rare shell. Looking closer, I realized it had come from that incongruous superstructure the oil platform out in the channel not far away, standing on gigantic steel pillars driven into the ocean floor and above the storm's reach.

Perhaps the red plastic thing was a reminder that imperfect man is part of perfect nature. Conjuring up the possibility seemed to ease my apprehension. I was making the effort to be objective—trying so hard to see beyond what I hoped would be only an interim, temporary encroachment of offshore oil drillers; I was trying to admire the power of the will of those modern miracle-workers. Despite these efforts, I could not avoid the more persistent underlying thought: one has to trust that in time, technical wonders and technical wonder-workers will absorb the destructive consequences of their efforts. More people must find their common cause with nature. This had been my thought even before ecologists started telling us that man had declared war on nature at the beginning of the Christian era, or perhaps even during the Neolithic culture.

These reflections were wrapped also in memories of what happened to farm machinery when it was left to the elements. Deteriorating, rusting implements—homemade inventions—had been a common sight in my childhood. It was an era of invention. Impressions like these must have sunk purposively into my conservative nature long ago, to prepare me for the present feelings of loss.

An enormous starfish, stranded temporarily on the beach by the minus tide, was repeating itself in the wet sand in squirming efforts to get back into the water. The sight brought to mind the fact of tides and cycles and seasons and the intricate, interlocking, big and small lives that since the beginning of time have been determined by them.

I was, by then, in spite of myself, siding with nature's genius against that of man as demonstrated in the enormous structure offshore. I was, without fully knowing, trying to escape a human fate that at the moment seemed far from desirable. I was instinctively, for survival, insinuating my small self into nature's grand scheme.

5

MERGING

~ LYNDA ~

When I returned to the ranch several years after it was sold, to begin the process of choosing the parcel my mother would buy back, I was jolted by the changes. The road had been paved, the deep turns into the canyons had been minimized, and fences had been added; a gate at the entrance was like a guard rather than a marker. There was a new, pleasant building, which was the office where the real estate plan was being developed and sales were being made. The orchards I had grown up with near my grandparents' house had been ripped out, and the livestock—horses and cattle—was gone.

The whole place felt cleaned up, sterilized. There was no horse or cow manure along the road. I learned that someone was responsible for keeping the road civilized looking, to create a quality that would be attractive to city people with a romantic yen to live on a historic old ranch. Such potential buyers would not want too much dust, or the stink of animal droppings, or openness to the wilderness. The developers thought it necessary to have locks, guards at the gate to check incoming traffic, and fences to hold back the unknown of nature.

I went to look at my grandparents' house, where I had spent so much of my childhood. It had always been known as the Big House, which was the usual name for the owners' house on a ranch, but the developers had renamed it "the mansion." The word choked me; I could not say it.

I went inside and felt dismayed. The house had, of course, been emptied, and it stood hollow and echoing as I walked through. The beautiful floors my grandmother had prized and would not let us children walk on were well preserved but bleak somehow without the fine Chinese rugs I remembered. I even missed Grandmother's anxious scrutiny of my movements through her living room. As Grandmother had made her children use the "children's entrance," allowing them to enter her part of the house only in soft shoes or socks, so did she instruct her grandchildren. Much as I had resented her constant harping about being careful not to hurt anything in her house, she was an intrinsic part of my memory, and I missed her now.

I remembered the house as a huge, solid, safe place. When I was young and new to the ranch, I would retreat into our children's part of the house when the effort to integrate with my cousins and the ranch ways became too exhausting. My room, which had been just to sleep in, was down the long hall beyond my grandparents' room, far from the children's quarters, and I remember feeling a bit anxious and tentative when, at night, I had to leave the relaxed warmth of my brother's and our nanny's rooms. But it was, nonetheless, a room of my own, with a high, comfortable bed and safely removed from the wilderness outside. Grandmother had created a civilized oasis in her house and garden, and since my life up to age seven had been in cities, her house was a fortress for me.

Now, after all had been sold, I saw her house for the first time with objective eyes and was saddened by how ordinary and empty it was. It was no longer big, or a fortress, or Grandmother's oasis. It had become just a house.

My mother had begun to look at the ranch with objective eyes thirty years after she left it to make her life in civilization. Twenty years after I had left it for the same reason, it was sold. For my mother, everything seemed changed after her father died, as it did for me after the ranch was sold. Yet, for us both, as we began to understand our relationship to the ranch the reality of the wilderness in that place began to draw us in. Somehow all the surface changes faded away, and we both found our way into the depths that were beyond change.

And how alive my memories still are! I remember the canyon beyond the house as a wonderful place, a place experienced from horseback. (So many of my memories center on horses!) With or without saddles, my cousins and I would ride up and over the rock wall that formed the falls. We would make a terrible racket, partly to drown out the fear we had climbing the rock wall. It was precipitous and high, and even though our horses were at home everywhere on the ranch, since they had been born there, we children did not feel secure.

Up above the falls it was like a park. Tall, leafy trees, the small stream, and an easy trail calmed us and quieted our noise. But as children we did not pay attention to natural noises or unnatural silences. Because we did not record our experiences or speak of them, my memories are impressionistic, felt rather than visualized. Our only grasp on that time was in the form of the "Remember when…?" storytellings we would engage in months or years later.

"Remember when we rode up the Bulito (the home canyon) and saw the rotten cow carcass in the creek above the water pipe?" This pipe brought our drinking water down to the house.

"Remember when you were scared to ride up the rock wall and had to lead your horse?" It was all right to lead your horse down the wall, but it was "sissy" to lead it up.

"Remember when we helped Joe (one of my mother's brothers) build the dam at the falls?" We had helped haul bags of cement mix up an elaborate pulley-and-platform system Joe had built up the rock wall.

Only on my return to the ranch after it had been sold did I begin really to see my surroundings; and only now, many years after that trip, am I beginning to think about what I observed.

I remember times alone on the ranch and the quiet that would surround me as I moved along a trail or over the hard, wet sand at the beach. Sometimes I would stop somewhere and sit, and after a while I would become half-drowsy and entranced. Then I would seem to meld into the setting, sink into the grass or sand, wriggle in until I fit into it rather than on it. Thinking and self-awareness would fade away, and I would float, seeing and hearing nothing at all.

I would never notice specific sights except sometimes if there was motion. To this day, I see very little objectively. I absorb my surroundings in some other way, and then only when I am alone. By blending into the landscape I have the landscape in me, but I cannot describe it, as my mother can. I *am* the landscape; and I feel rested and fed as a result.

This experience, which I call "merging," is the heart of my relationship with the wilderness. I find I have to feel alone to merge, so that I can make an intimate connection with the wilderness, with myself as a creature of nature, and with the sense of awe that is the hallmark of the Other, the reality that is greater than oneself. I can feel alone in this way when others are around, but only if there is no talking. When I go out entirely alone, however, I am always anxious too. But this is anxiety caused by awe of the enormity of the wilderness bringing home to me my vulnerability and frailty, not the anxiety of loss. As my mother says, you know you do not have answers, only a constant questioning: What is that sound? What is that rustle? What is making those grasses move? One way of calming my anxiety is to stop and sit and be very still. This gives me an opportunity to secure my immediate surroundings, to determine who else is there with me: what bird, what insect, what lizard. I can usually be sure that any larger creature—deer, coyote, snake—will move away from me. Sitting gives me a certain territoriality, and I can begin to relax. Except for the bites of bugs or ticks, the buzzing of flies or mosquitos, nothing will bother me, most likely. So then I can begin to meld into the surroundings in the twilight state that is the prelude to merger. It is easier to slide into it on a warm, quiet day, because there is little or no difference between my body temperature and the air temperature. Being still reduces my awareness of my body, so I can drift. Drifting takes me into the merger, a thoughtless flowing, a floating, a union with the setting. I do not know I am merged; I do not know anything.

Only when something flaps or runs or makes a noise do I become specifically aware of it. Then I do see the wave of the white tip of a fox's tail as he speeds up the bank off the beach. I see the young bald eagle, flapping clumsily away from home to start his own life. I look for the big crow squawking overhead. But mainly I sink into unconsciousness and namelessness and flow along in the wild.

Growing up on the ranch, I found a special kind of merger through animals. On horseback, and especially while pushing a great herd of cattle down the beach, merger came easily. Much of the cattle work was done in the summer, so the slow procedure of nudging a herd along between the ocean and the cliffs was done under a hot sun. The heavy sun bearing down, the soft splashing of the summer waves, the cattle swishing flies off their backs, and the monotonous whistles of the men all contributed to a lulling of my perceptions. Together with the easy plodding of the horse, these things would lead me into the somnolence and floating that was merger with the environment. Again, I would be aware of my state only after being jolted to consciousness, perhaps by my horse's stumbling over his own feet, a consequence of his somnolence. Or sometimes it would be a shout from one of the men to alert me to the fact that some cow had stopped and I had ridden on past her in my half-sleep. Jerking awake, I would look back to where the cowboy was pointing and feel embarrassed to see the cow standing still and watching me ride away. Coming back to the herd with the cow trotting ahead of me, I would realize how far gone I had been and resolve to stay on my toes and not let it happen again. But after another mile or so, the langor would creep over me again. It was wonderful and terrible both, the power of that merging.

I learned early that such a way of being must be backed up by a capacity to come to instant consciousness when in the wilderness. The sudden presence of a threat—a rattlesnake or some other danger—requires reflexes rather than deliberation. On a cattle drive, I might be jolted to alertness by one of the men, but while riding alone, I sometimes found myself being yanked out of merger by being thrown onto the hard ground! A horse, too, can be half asleep when something shocks it—a rabbit jumping up, a sudden breeze moving a branch, its own stumbling over a rock—and it is all too easy to fall off if the horse jumps. More than once I have found myself coming to consciousness a hair too late and having to walk long miles down a canyon to get home, my horse having disappeared ahead of me.

When we were children, merger with the land was a physical as well as psychological involvement. I remember especially a winter of extremely heavy rains and endless mud. Everything was slick and boggy; horses could not keep their footing, and cars were useless. The roads were impassable because of the adobe; even chains could not cope with the gumminess.

That winter of the rains, we played in the swollen, muddy-banked creeks and were drawn into them literally. There was something fascinating about trying to keep our footing on the rocky bottom while the water swirled and threw us off balance. As a result, it was an important thing to have boots to the knee. My city galoshes were a laughing matter, and I was teased so much that I finally prevailed upon Grandmother to get me knee boots, too. With high boots, we could go way out and see how near the tops of the boots the water would come. Always the water came over the tops and filled around our feet. It was unpleasant at first because the water was so cold, but after a while our feet would warm up the water, so a little more would not hurt. Often we would fall in and get soaked. If it happened near the bank, such a fall would mean being coated with black adobe mud. Scraping it off with our fingers spread it further. The obvious next thing was to smear each other, and soon we would be in a full-fledged mud fight. These were horrible in a way—mud in the face, hair, and clothes, cold and sticky—but at the same time exhilarating: there was nothing more to lose. We became one with our environment.

The reason my memory of those cold, wet, muddy times is so clear is that the nanny looking after my brother and me made me take a galvanized bucket of cold water and wash out my jeans on the lawn. I could get only the main lumps out, of course, but the process brought awareness of the experience. The unpleasant job of outdoor cold-water washing did not, however, induce me to stop playing in the creeks and the mud with the others. We were like a bunch of otters in our mud-sliding and playing.

The beach was another place that drew us in. The wintry creeks and mud were cold and slimy, but the summer beach was warm and dry. When we were very young we spent long, anonymous days there, the white-starched nanny reading and sleeping in the shade of the cliff that bordered the coastline for miles in both directions.

Miss Annis would settle herself at the base of the cliff, out of the wind, and we would leave her there. We would check for her now and then during the day, but she seemed never to move. Her white-uniformed figure lay motionless alongside our small heaps of clothes; I think she mostly slept.

We would head straight for the waves, naked as jaybirds. I do not know how long it took me to learn to swim. Certainly no one taught me. I would try to stay inshore of the waves and pretend to swim in the wash, kicking my feet and walking on my hands. The pull of the waves was frightening at first, but with time I became more at ease, and it was not too long before I could follow the others. We would let the wash pull us back to the next wave and duck under it as it fell or dive through its curve, coming out behind it. A game was to line up in a row and ride a wave in as seals would, only our heads sticking out in the tube formed by the falling water, shouting to each other in the moment before we went under.

The water was icy cold, however, and finally even we knew we were too cold. Teeth chattering, we would race up to the hot, dry sand and burrow down into its delicious warmth. With no suits to get scratchy with sand, we could wriggle and dig our way down until finally we were warm.

Then would come a sort of trance state, during which we might just lie quietly or smooth a space in front of us to draw on with one finger. Or we would begin to dig a tunnel to the person lying nearest and try to meet fingers underneath.

There would be a sort of humming in the air made up of warm sun, hot sand, birds making their various noises, and the waves rising and falling. It was a strange, timeless condition, and one of the rare times of harmony among us all.

So it was doubly jolting when worldly events would intrude. Even though it happened twice a day, every day, the appearance of Southern Pacific's Daylight train on its way between San Francisco and Los Angeles was always such an event. We would jump up and, entirely oblivious of our nakedness, wave at the train. The passengers, waving back at us, seemed so friendly; but years later it occurred to me that they were fascinated by our nakedness. This was during World War II, in the early 1940s, and even children did not play on the beach without something on.

One day, though, something happened that was unencompassable. Lying warm and somnolent in the dry sand, we were watching two gull-winged trainer planes fly around just above the kelp line. On that day the kelp was quite close in, maybe half a mile offshore. The planes seemed to be playing follow the leader. Single engine, each plane had one man in it. Perhaps the pilots were preparing to fly fighter planes for the navy.

Suddenly, one plane flew too low and caught its propellor in the kelp. The tail flipped up in the air and the plane stood briefly on its nose, then slid underwater.

By now we were standing at the edge of the waves, stunned. No one said anything. We watched and watched, but no one appeared in the water. The other plane circled several times over the spot where the first plane had disappeared, then flew off toward Santa Barbara.

We did not speak of it. We lay back down in the sand and reentered the trance state that I associate with this beach of my childhood. We absorbed the incident as we absorbed every shocking event; little was made of calamities. Life went on.

6

Corral Work at Las Cruces Ranch

~ JANE ~

The wild will not be captured—at least not by man. Two aspects of that thought were demonstrated on my trip to the ranch in March 1962. The colors of spring and the old-time cattle work both made themselves felt in a new way for me. Never before had I seen their power to engage me, nor the way in which they could not be grasped. Colors on the ranch could be waylaid only in glimpses, if they were to be grasped at all. They were not to be pinned down. Like the wind, they were gone in the moment and became their own experience. Wild animals that have grown used to man are no longer wild animals. Like us, they lose their perfection. They are no longer the Other. They have come into consciousness and no longer have the mysterious quality of a dream.

Wildflowers grown in our gardens are the same. Nature is of the moment, necessarily fleeting, or it is not nature—its colors most of all. I found myself having to return to the scene as though by some magnetic pull, having to breathe it in, dwell on it for as long as possible, stay by with riveted eyes, but always return. I had to find out, finally, that flowers will not come away with you. You go back and back again to them for renewal—that is the point.

On the night of my arrival on the ranch at the end of March 1962, I was confronted by the wind. From out there in the dark the wind literally greeted me the moment I stepped out of the car at the Gaviota store, our telephone exchange and source of supplies as well as the pooling center for gossip for miles around. The wind carried to me the faintest confusion of scents from what turned out to be a tangle of colors and life and peaceful exuberance. That night, in its continuous movement the wind was like a wild thing. Fresh and cold and strong, it was saying something—something about a past still living in the present.

For years, the wind had stung our eyes with the dirt it carried from traveled roads and from bare places around the buildings. I remembered especially how it had roiled up the soil in corrals pulverized by our ever-moving horses. The fine dust would become soft, gray masks for our faces. That night in March, however, ensconced in the superintendent's home (he and his wife had given me a standing invitation to stay with them whenever I came to the ranch), I knew something was being added. Memories of the wind, an inseparable childhood companion, were coming to life. The wind had been more than a trial: it had been an integral part of our coast ranch. It had also been a symbol, even in its violence. For the first time I realized that, without the wind, our place would not have been our place. Too many days of quiet would have been debilitating.

In some ways, the wind had been our protector. It had driven away those who disliked its disturbing ways. The wind literally had insured the original quality of our coast. I do not wonder now that Vizcaíno, in 1602, had called it *Punta de la Limpia Concepción* (Point of the Immaculate Conception). Thanks to the wind, it was indeed untouched.

When I opened my bedroom window that night in the superintendent's snug board-and-batten house, the wind, by then quietened, nosed around the house wanting to visit. And it had something more on its mind: it was insinuating for my benefit that the past few weeks of too many people and too much talk in the city need not have been.

Sleep came slowly because of the tension built up by too much city life and issues about the future of the ranch. The periodic tiny crashes on the roof from falling eucalyptus seeds and the sound of their wayward rolling in the wind also kept me from sleep: I was kept awake savoring these long-forgotten and comforting thumps in the night.

On the ranch road that evening, a soft, furry thing had slipped into the tall mustard beside the road; it had been only a bare suggestion, a pale, vague impression, but my alerted senses had told me it must have been a young coyote. Another old friend also had been on the road: a skunk, a fellow commanding respect not only for his lethal weapon and intelligence but also because he is discriminating. He does not let fly if he knows you. He had loped clumsily before me. It had been a treat to see him in the headlights, outlined against the pale, dusty road. His broad, white stripe and full tail as long as his body had marked him as one of the large variety.

A phone call in the morning, rudely knocking me out of my daydreaming, changed everything about my mood. There would be a branding party at Las Cruces Ranch; friends of the family, neighboring ranchers, and hangers-on would be there. Exhibition roping, drinks, and all that. Scents and sounds and colors and new resolutions promised by the wind in the night would have to wait, unless I could steal some time for myself on the way.

I was expected to go to the branding party. "They" would never understand that I had been looking forward all month to two days of nothing coming between the wild coast and me. Besides, as a member of the ranch's board of directors, it was my job to look over the '62 calves and help decide whether the cow-calf operation should be continued. The board had been considering a recommendation by the experts that we maintain only as many cows as we could feed in a drought year and, depending on how much more rain fell, buy stockers each year to fill out our herd. We might be realistic and use drought conditions as the baseline for our thinking.

This was advice the Chumash had laid down in their myths long before experts had ever been heard of. In a yearly contest before the rainy season, Sun and Eagle were on one side. If they won, they ate people, and Sun hoarded the world's goods. If the other side, Morning

Star and Šnilemun (Coyote of the Sky) won, they let fall all the world's goods that Sun had been hoarding. Moon was referee. The Chumash, unlike us, had taken droughts for granted. We, always taken unaware, had never accepted them as a normal part of our living. We were taught to believe God is good!

On the way to Las Cruces, I deliberately took time to be alone with my observations: '62 was definitely developing into a poppy-and-clover year. In early spring, we always named the current year according to what was growing plentifully. It might be named for a flower or a grass or some rodent that had multiplied out of proportion to nature's balance, or, negatively, for an epidemic. The "Year of the Rat" on the Chinese calendar in 1960 had been no surprise to me.

One year, before the era of machines, had been named for the locust. "Remember the year of the locusts?" still rings in my ears. For days, so long ago, the air had been dense with hopping, flying locusts pelting us from all directions. Men had driven horse teams onto the grainfields on the mesas dragging scoops of crude oil in an effort to catch the insects before they mopped up every living, growing thing in sight. I was very young at the time, but I remember it as though it happened last week; I still feel the intolerable heat and see the grain stalks being stripped to the ground. The horses never stopped tossing their heads as millions of locusts pelted them and fell into the black oil. Relentlessly the locusts came—clouds upon clouds of them—until suddenly they were no more. And not a blade of grass was to be seen anywhere.

On the coast ranch, before turning inland to Las Cruces, I noticed that the poppies on the bare, white shale banks were unusually large. In the bright morning, the flowers glowed. I stopped the car to look. Sunlight, penetrating the petals, was making them transparent. Sun and poppy petals were all one: tiny orange flames, petals full of sun. Words would not come. I was seeing the poppies for the first time.

As I looked back to the San Augustine's coastal bluffs, I saw that the natural gas that escaped wastefully from the Texaco installation was on fire. The flame, suspended so far away in the bright morning sky, was still another poppy.

In the Llegua (from the Spanish *yegua*, "mare," and third canyon west of the Bulito), red brome and its fierce cousin, ripgut, were still green and tall and luxuriant beside the road, not betraying their deadly summer role. Seeded heads heavy and bending under their weight, their green blades reflected the sun.

It was quiet, surprisingly quiet. The wind was not around to insinuate itself into my life today. Sage flowers were everywhere, tiers upon tiers of soft, lavender petals on long, stiff, gray vertical sprays. Young mustard—yellow from the late second growth, defying the cattle—gracefully swept the soft, round hills in the distance farther east, subduing the deep orange poppies in its intense green undercoat. Large sun-yellow daisies with their dark, earth-brown centers showed up beside the soft lavender of the black sage and the darker purple of the morning glory. Outsized Indian paintbrushes, already fattened and feathered, turned true red against the poppies.

It was hard to find words to fit the colors. Colors had meant little to me in my youth. I like to think that this oversight had been partly in reaction to the exaggerated and, what seemed to me, affected, responses of visitors from the city. More likely, it had been a child's narrow outlook. A visitor myself this time, and lacking the words to hold off the impact, I was completely taken over. I felt a need to make these colors my own, if possible, to make up for the lost time.

Form had always mattered to me in the past: structure and balance and proportion as they manifest in warm-blooded life or in sculptured mountains, interesting shapes, boulders, smooth river rock, cliff out-lines. The characteristic, confirming shapes and ritualized movements of wildlife and the strong shapes of the men of labor were what I remembered mostly. So many of my impressions had been tones, including those of the men. I had always been at home with shapes and movements; they had served as my basis for judgment. In fact, the movements of the ranch wildlife are so deeply imprinted in my consciousness that to this day the slightest movement of an animal immediately tells me what its species is. Had I been destined to be an artist, I would have been a sculptor. Because color was not part of my awareness, it became important only when the ranches were threat-ened.

On my way to the rodeo, I took notes in order somehow to control this color crisis. This one is redder than that one; it has more blue in it, or yellow; or that one is somehow different. This glows; that one is subtler. Then I tried analogies: the paintbrushes were like fat, color-book exclamation points in a field run amok with color. But my descriptive efforts were disappointing. I thought, then, Do these colors go together? If we plant them in our gardens, they do not. But all colors in nature go together always. In wild places they blend; they add, subtract, emphasize; sometimes they subdue.

I had to admit that there is nothing under the sun like a flower! The word that reaches directly for a particular flower color in itself simply does not exist!

I was a child again, learning to walk. I could, however, ferret out one attribute that helped explain the difficulty: wild colors, like wild scents and all wild phenomena, wild animals especially, are characteristically fleeting—in a way, that is what "wild" means.

Possession is possible only in one's own changing—in the realization of one's achieved difference. Change comes insofar as you are possessed by nature, as I was possessed this day by her colors. You must make the effort to become a small part of the wild. But you cannot hold within your boundaries what extends to infinity. You have, however, to struggle to stretch those boundaries a little, if you can. And when you are old, perhaps you will reach as far as your infinity intends for you.

A disturbing thought intruded itself: Had my boundaries already extended long ago beyond that small amount, to my disadvantage and without my knowing? And perhaps I was only now realizing the outward pull of those boundaries and facing the task of concentrating myself back into my certain size through the efforts of forcing out the appropriate words? But then, whatever the problem, it was mine. That much was certain. The colors had always been there.

A morning glory, its petals thrown wide, victoriously topped a black sage bush high against the open sky. Successfully maneuvering a long, canny climb into the light, it had become a white-bright, triumphant contrast to the soft green-gray around it.

The large clumps with bell-type flowers that I remembered still dominated the road with their soft, dark, almost midnight blue. They might have escaped from a cultivated garden.

In spite of the developing heat, the clean air was like a substance. I could have eaten it. It was animated, barely stirring, with the slightest suggestion of the past winter cool in it.

Around noontime at Agua Caliente Canyon, just before I turned inland onto the short stretch of highway leading to Las Cruces, fog encroached from the sea in wraithlike, insubstantial wisps. It poured hurriedly onto the shore, where the hot sun, already entrenched, beat it back. The fog would not be put down. A struggle developed. I drove on slowly, enjoying being caught in the middle. All along, vistas opened and closed in rapid succession. Orange velvet poppies closed against the oppressive heat of the sudden midday stillness. The heavy atmosphere was pushing down from above.

Past noon, finally, I arrived at the rodeo corrals near the entrance to Las Cruces. Not bad, considering I had only ten miles to travel and had been expected to be there by ten o'clock.

Inside the "diamond" that was Las Cruces Ranch, the land was lush and green and sparkling that day, without the slightest sound of traffic. The surrounding hills, protectively cutting off the outside world, made it a quiet, hot, and sleepy place, perfect for the corrals and the rodeo.

As in the past, the branding, although essential to the cattle operation, was a jocular event. Strong men competed in games of risk and skill—roping, branding, cutting—not forgetting, however, that it was their way to make a living and that they could never relax their concern for the cattle. They must get the animals out onto the range and back to normal as soon as possible.

It was not always easy to lower the brand right side up on the sprawling, bawling calf, and the men were not young. They had been at it a week, dawn to dark and Sunday too: twelve hours just the day before. There was a continuous undercurrent of good humor, and masculine exclusivity, in their commentary: "Oh, it's only a heifer!" for the one that got away.

It was a good show, for skill is always the thing; yet with all the laughter ("joshing," they called it) the vaqueros were more tense than I remembered them being in my father's time. We had had no outsiders looking on in those days.

Some guests wandered clumsily, picnic baskets and drinks in hand. A few clung to the massive corral fence boards, but not for long. Others peered briefly into the dust and confusion, not seeing the occasional big moments of daring and expertise in the now almost-forgotten art. Most of the guests stood around among themselves. They were people "at a rodeo," who had not ridden day after day nor eaten the dust in the corrals with the smell of burning hair in their noses and spurts of blood spattering them, occasionally having to ride out a colt who bucked in rebellion at the confusion. They had not, day in and day out, borne the din of the incessant bawling of the calves and the long, anxious calls of the cows. They had not felt the fatigue and put up with long hours of grime and smoke from the fire that heated the irons.

The cattleman does not understand too well the city man's beady-eyed consciousness, his egotism. Under this kind of scrutiny, he will drift into a state of being there and at the same time not there. He has a talent for camouflage, a self-possession that blends him into his surroundings. The real cattleman does not want to be noticed. He might have learned his disappearing act from the Indians; more likely it comes out of his adjustment to the wilderness.

I was reminded of the time a Navajo, his head turned away, had refused to look a white man in the eyes as he answered questions. The white man's ego had been for him somehow distasteful; possibly the Navajo was not able to stand it. Our vaqueros were, in a way, like that, made so by life with the elements. That was something I understood well. Maintaining so low a profile, as the modern phrase goes, that you are not seen at all, was second nature to me. I remember once being startled, but also grateful, when a sophisticated lady in Europe told me I had a talent for making myself invisible.

Our cattlemen were proud and aloof. They not only earned a wage, they also had the dignity of men of labor; they were products of daily challenge from working alone in isolated places. The size of our ranches made that necessary. They had a humility that, in their milieu, came from having constantly to prove themselves. Their humility came out of a respect for the bigness of nature, of having taken their places within the realm of overpowering forces. Their firm step and deliberate movements, their physical coordination, proved what they were.

In the early days ours had been a working ranch; and that term, "working ranch," had signified so much. It had been our password. The ranch had been a human affair—something to be proud of. When machines were introduced our pride was cut down, and I wonder, now, what happened to the animals. Better than average management makes a small profit in good years in California, but only with the help of accountants and machines and the general depersonalization that goes with them. Agribusiness, they call it. My father had not been sufficiently impressed with the concept, and that is why we had to sell out once he was gone. Our operation lost too much money. Progress in our society, unfortunately, was measured quantitatively, by the amount of money we made, not by the aboriginal measurements I shared with my father—namely, the increase of quality, whether in our product or in our individual expertise.

That day at the branding, nevertheless, the two groups in their unhappy symbiosis somehow carried on, the city people oblivious of the ranch people and the ranch people with their backs turned. The city was severed from its connection with the country, like a head from its body.

The vaqueros continued with their efforts—a small cluster off to one side of the corral tending the animals. Ribald jokes were lost under their wide hats. The "polo crowd," as the city group called themselves, filled the surrounding stage with comings and goings between drinks, their talk grating on unrelated to the purpose of the day—a preview of what was to come. In another decade the working roundup would no longer exist, and few people would even notice that it had gone. Rodeos on commercial scales would continue in brutal blatancy to cash in on the western tradition. Rootless men from ranches no longer able to make a living would gather at jackpot competitions, traveling from place to place for the money. They already rode "outlaws" trained by means of goads to buck, roping the miserable calves bought for the purpose. In such a situation, vis-à-vis the animal, man becomes the enemy. The animal is thus degraded beyond recognition or turned renegade; that is what we now call a "bronc show." Man's inner animal (his instinct) also has to turn renegade to match the creatures he has created.

It was already too late for some of us; we could never fit into what was happening. The "wild thing" contained in our ranch-bred horses, in the men who trained them, and in the cattle would always be there in its pure potency, at least for me, if only in a depressed lump inside. I felt sad for our lost city people, blindly trying to find their animal roots in an experience the cattlemen had, without understanding that that was what they had come for. If only each group could realize what the other one was about and how much they will need each other. The cattlemen will be cast adrift too, once the ranches are gone.

At that thought, my old feeling of imminent loss of our ranches returned. It was a pull back to reality.

How often does one have to go through the sense of loss, I wondered, to make it one's own in order to grow beyond it? And then what? The "wild thing," no longer with a physical space to nourish it and gone for good, would have to be found inwardly to cope with the ever-returning, gnawing nostalgia. Once experienced in childhood, it simple will not be put down. Or would a thicker protective skin be the answer? And what about a society that needs a thick skin? If my feeling for nature could be suppressed, why did I continue to try to mend my primitive-modern split? But I seemed to have no choice. Besides, someday, I hoped, knowing and honoring the wild within or without would help me, no matter where, to feel my rootedness.

These two disconnected groups, city people and country people, do not come together knowingly. But they may be driven together by secret forces concerned with the future. For me, further exposure to the wild, to the ranch as it was, would help me be more articulate about that future. And there was time. It would take several years to dispose of five ranches in one piece to avoid the double tax.

The scene at the branding corral at Las Cruces nevertheless stayed with me; I continued to wonder at it. The scene had not added to my efforts to date to assimilate my wilderness heritage so that it would not interfere with the eventual need to return to civilization. The jarring note that day instead had discouraged my delving for the time being. The activity at the branding corrals had showed a glaring difference between city life and life in undisturbed wild places.

I would have preferred to join the working crew, as I always had in the many years I had spent on the ranch. Unhappily, it had not been possible; I had had to side with the guests. But then, what about my preference? The "outsiders" had upset my rapport with nature. But why should they have? Why couldn't I have held my own? Was so delicate a balance of nature involved? My reflection no longer functioned; is nature, then, a state of mind, not a thing in itself? But we know that left to her own devices nature, when disturbed by whatever elemental force, restores her balance. So, then, is nature on the "inside" more fleeting than she is out there? And what of one's childhood imprinting? Where does that take us? Certainly, imprinting becomes a faithful mirror of the outside, even though at times it functions inappropriately.

Much later, I wondered if all humans have a psychic layer that, given a chance, exactly corresponds to untouched wilderness and could manifest as man's potential delight in wilderness and potential ability to survive in it. The ecologists say: if wilderness goes, man goes. Are they perhaps unknowingly referring to this psychic layer in humans? Are they inadvertently pointing out nature's balancing power as the survival ingredient in all of us? In that case, if we do not honor and experience the wilderness outwardly, we cannot find that inward healing, balancing level in ourselves. The resulting imbalance will doom us.

The human animal originally evolved within the context of wilderness; our biological roots are therefore mostly wilderness oriented. Modern evolutionary charts indicate that our prehistoric development was at least ninety-nine percent of our total development. Psychic evolution developed as part of the biological. Without psychic and biological roots, the human being is unable to survive. We need a minimum of contact with wilderness to reconnect with our billions of years of evolutionary existence in wilderness. Like a tree, we must have roots or die—if not physically, at least spiritually. In psychology, maintaining balance had been termed "resolving the opposites"; as far as I can see, the same goes for finding a balance between the experiences of city and nature.

Experiencing wilderness has to be a two-way process of outer physical connection and psychic reflection, so tenuous it can function only in quiet and stillness and in the rhythm of natural movement, regardless of how violent are the ordering elemental forces of nature. One must brook no interference from people, no matter how pliant they are. An Indian might be an exception. No one else.

Nature's self-containment forces one to be the observer registering everything, no matter how big or small, violent or peaceful. Only then can the wilderness within match the wilderness without. Humans, though privileged, are only a vehicle for such a happening. And even then, I believe, the vehicle may work only if nature is experienced early in life.

This inner-outer balance is an ancient Oriental way of meeting life; but it was absent that day at the ranch. I had been saddened by the "polo crowd," who had not been exposed to the wilderness early in life and so had lost their capacity for awe.

After the branding, I drove into the back country of Las Cruces for a quick look, in hopes of shaking off the heat of the corrals and the conflicts of the day. The ranch, cloaked in a thick coat of green, was cooled by a fresh breeze. The breeze came and went; it was on and off. A communicative meadowlark, a shrill red-winged blackbird, and a linnet with his querying song were the only signs of life other than that of the laboring creek close by. Like all other creeks everywhere, it was strong and clear. "The rich passivity of nature"* was never so evident.

In the evening light on the coast road, going home, the slanting sun rays penetrated the yellow of the mustard, turning it into deep gold. The wind was full and substantial, more determined than on Las Cruces. On

---

* Robert Louis Stevenson, *Silverado Squatters* (Ashland, OR: Lewis Osborne, 1972), 104.

foot, I turned into Coyote Canyon just west of the Sacate, wanting to prolong my time alone. The Coyote is aptly named, for there are nearly always coyotes there. Light lingered on the hills, and the wind was in the power lines that cut across the mouth of the canyon, making them sound like ship's rigging. The humming made the ocean seem all the nearer. Frogs were beginning to assert themselves. Their croaks were scattered and individual; the chorus would come later. The stream's lonely self-absorption pleased me. A small group of Mexican cattle was bedding down in the tall grass. Into the canyon the wind funneled coldly from the north. Giant rye nestled in the land creases up on the ridge. Rye is what the Chumash Indians used for baskets and, some say, for arrow shafts. For us, grasses were indications of seepage and potential springs.

At the first rock ledges I had to detour widely around a bog to find a way through rank grass that was tough enough when trod on to serve as a raft over the deep, watery mud. A crazy quilt of hoofprints marked the bog where the "Mexicans" had been holding a convention.

I wanted to breathe the air as though I would never breathe again. It tasted clean and good, and I needed to take it in, to have it always.

Back in the car and around the first bend, I saw the San Augustine's bluff far away. The gas flame on the Texaco installation, no longer a poppy, became a lesser setting sun that had mistakenly slipped back over the ocean to where the big sun had set the January before. The sun's spring position, halfway to the ridge that marked the place of the summer solstice, impressed me with how wide the sun's arc is.

7

INSIDERS, OUTSIDERS, AND BELONGING

~ LYNDA ~

My mother's description of the branding party is from the position of "belonging" to the ranch. Since I did eventually come to belong, I can appreciate her frustration with having to be with the guests and thus be cut off from the ranch people. One could not do both at the same time. But I also identify with the guests and their situation as outsiders.

I remember my first roundup, which took place perhaps a month after my arrival on the ranch as a child. Actually it was the work in the corrals I was taken to watch. A huge herd of cows and calves had been brought in, with the purpose of branding and sorting and weaning the calves.

One step was to castrate the little bull calves. The parts that the men cut off the calves were placed on the stones at the edge of the branding-iron fire to cook. Subsequently, one or another of my ranch-born cousins would take one of these delicacies and eat it. Sometimes a trickle of blood and juice would appear on his or her mouth and chin.

After this first branding event, I would run when my cousins chased me because I thought they wanted to eat me, too.

When my brother and I appeared on the ranch, aged four and seven, respectively, our three cousins reacted to us as if we were aliens. John

53

and I arrived on the ranch in late spring, on the last leg of a long trip from Europe, where our family had lived for the previous six years. I was very disoriented. Combined with the effects of dust and heat was a severe nausea brought on by the ten miles of rough, curving road that wove in and out of the big canyons after it left the highway. As we came down into Bulito Canyon, where the Big House was, I saw what seemed to be a civilized area of trees, lawns, and garden surrounding a huge house, with vegetable gardens and orchards extending beyond toward the ocean. But as we drew near to the house there was a sudden caterwauling, and three wild faces appeared at the car windows. I remember shrinking farther into the back seat and watching in horror as these apparitions sorted themselves out into three children, one about my age and two quite a bit older, who had jumped onto the running boards of our moving car in order to get a look at us. They shouted and gestured, and I could understand nothing about them. It was as if they had dropped out of the trees. They were my cousins, born and bred to the ranch.

For the next few years, I knew nothing but that I was afraid of the three children who "belonged" and that I had a powerful, unarticulated drive to get in with them. My brother made a different decision. He developed a separate life and had no contact with the group. When he was old enough he took off on long, solitary walks, and we never saw him.

My effort to be included by the other children was unremitting and lasted about five years. Toward the end of that period I began to feel a little safer and even welcome, sometimes. After that five-year span I "belonged," more or less. Once I was secure, it was worth every terrifying, anguished incident, but the process of getting there was made infinitely harder because I did not know if I would ever make it. Actually, I could not even have said what my goal was.

Those five years are a blur now, punctuated by sharp memories. There was the first horse ride, perhaps days after I arrived. My mother's three brothers all had houses on the ranch, built in the same canyon where my grandmother and grandfather had built in 1911. My three cousins were the children of two of these brothers. I remember going up to my uncle Jack's house and being boosted onto the bare back of a round, black Shetland pony named Charlie. Charlie hated us all and, being uncontrollable, made us pay for his feelings. I remember that first trip on Charlie as a race around the house, over a rough lawn, and under a date palm tree, dodging various obstacles while everyone hollered things at me. I do not know how many times we circled the house before Charlie had had enough. Nor do I know if I finally fell off. I do remember being bent over his neck, clinging with arms and legs. I was scared senseless.

I remember one day asking a cousin if I could ride behind her on her Dartmoor pony, Pyrene. I asked not because I wanted this ride but because I wanted to be included. The two girls were about three years older than the third cousin, Jimmy, and I, and they had been promoted from Shetlands to Dartmoors. My cousin agreed so quickly that I was afraid of her intent, and, sure enough, I was bucked off as soon as I got on. She laughed. I can see now that it was funny, but at the time I was offended and embarrassed.

We all were allowed finally to ride the cow horses, and this did make riding easier. Grandfather had a quarter horse stallion and a band of good-looking, though ordinary, brood mares. The young horses had grown up on the ranch and thus were secure in their footing on all its different terrains. So we were allowed access to a few of these horses. Mostly older and no longer used for the hardest cattle work, they were a wise bunch. They knew at once how inexperienced we were, how afraid, or how weak, and promptly took advantage of us. They did not pull the tricks the Shetlands knew, such as scraping us off under a branch or ripping our pants and legs by traveling too close to a barbed wire fence. They did not go into the middle of a creek and roll in the water, leaving us to scramble off before our legs were caught underneath them. They did, however, share the Shetlands' tendency to run away. Part of the danger of being run away with was losing one or both reins, leaving you with no means of control whatsoever. You could only hope that someone else would race even faster and grab the runaway's bridle or that the runaway would get bored with running and stop after a while.

Most worrisome of all was that the horse might step on the reins and come crashing down.

If a horse ran away on the beach, there was less danger because he would be contained by the cliffs and the footing was reliable. When a horse ran away on land, however, there was a great risk of his putting a foot into a gopher hole or falling over something. Only after a number of these wild rides did I discover—no one told me anything; that was part of the initiation process—that I had to pull one rein in until the horse's nose was practically back to my knee. Then he could run only in circles, and necessarily slowly enough that I could finally stop him. At last the day came when my horse was more or less under my control, but that took a number of years of constant riding, plus getting taller and heavier and more confident. And even then I had to keep a constant vigil lest the horse sense an opening to seize control again.

My daily sense of things was: Now I must go out and face today's trials. It was as though I had to pass an infinite number of tests, not only doing various feats but also developing an appearance of fearlessness. I was always afraid, but it was my job to conceal my fear and, in spite of it, do the terrifying thing. And for years, my cousins thought up new things to test me with.

These tests were all physical things, with an unspoken requirement to endure taunts, goads, and demolishing judgments without complaints or tears. I had arrived at the ranch able to read, write, and conceptualize. I could, at seven, do the usual city things, such as interact with people, ride a bike, dress in a city way. Such learning was irrelevant on the ranch and, in fact, gave rise to jeers and scorn. What was necessary to know there was how to handle your body without thinking, so that you could interact automatically with the environment. You needed not to think things through; rather, you had to come up with the right reaction immediately. As I have said, there was little talking. Doing was everything.

When my cousins were irritated with me, or bored, they would run away, often leaving me in unfamiliar places to find my way home alone. This was the hardest thing for me when I was new to the ranch, being run away from. We would go off together to some new place, and then my cousins would just disappear. It would be for me to find my way home. Being a stranger to the ranch was hard enough, but the feeling of being abandoned was worse. I was not yet used to the incredible solitude, and I was totally persuaded by the horror stories my cousins told of mountain lions, rattlesnakes, black widow spiders, and scorpions. Behind every bush I saw a lion, and in every hole in the ground, snakes and insects. I felt as though I would surely be eaten, or at least bitten, by something.

They would tempt me to do things that could not be done: pick prickly pears, jump from too high a place, ride a horse that would throw anyone but an adult. They would lead me places: up a tall tree, into a wild canyon, out beyond the breakers before I could swim. Sometimes I would refuse, eliciting shouts of triumph; other times I would try, and hurt myself. That was funny to them too.

On rainy days, I would wake up with a sigh of relief. There would be a respite until perhaps their mothers could not stand them indoors anymore. But eventually they would come past the Big House, where I lived with my grandparents, calling and teasing about my being a sissy and staying in out of the rain. So I would dress in rain gear and join them for adventures in the mud and cold.

Going to the one-room schoolhouse in Santa Anita Canyon, three miles away, was another scary process. We rode on the car's running boards, of course. No one would ride inside the car except the "little kids"—my brother and several other small cousins. We older ones leaned way out over the drop-offs beside the road, holding the roof edge with one hand. We walked forward and back, traded places, crouched down, and stood on one foot, all on the running board. Ultimately I felt safe doing this, but it took a very long time to arrive at that security.

When it rained we were taken to school on a tractor, or, if it was really pouring, we rode horseback—mostly on Shetlands and Dartmoors. My cousins would make their horses lean back on their haunches and slide, more or less gracefully, down to the bottom of the canyons. But Charlie would keep his rear high in the air so that I fell forward over his ears. If I had a saddle, that would slide onto his neck until finally he would stop, or start running down the hill, or buck me off.

At the bottom of one canyon the creek had dug a trench, and the ponies had to jump over it. All of them would, of course, except Charlie. Finally I would have to lead him over it, or, more ignominious, one of the others would ride him over. Then we had to crawl up the other side of the canyon, and my saddle or I would slide backward over Charlie's rump. Sometimes when he felt me back there he would hop forward and dump me on the path. Then he would run away, and one of the others would catch him, handing him back to me with more comments about my stupidity.

It took me many years to understand the difference between stupidity and ignorance. And I have never felt friendly toward Shetland ponies.

I gained acceptance by the cousins gradually. After a couple of years of trials, I began to feel less set apart. As I found my way into the group, I was finding my way into the depth of the ranch too, and that may have been a ticket of admission to the group. I am not sure which came first, and I am inclined to think they were simultaneous processes. I think that without that terrible struggle to join the cousins I would not have found my true relation to nature, since that sort of relation seems to be automatic only up to age four or five, and I was past that when I came to live on the ranch. Even as I remember the animal level of terror that I endured as a child, I realize what an extraordinary benefit it is to me to be able, quite deliberately, to merge with nature, partly as a result of that experience.

The final piece of this struggle to belong—not only to the group but also to the ranch—was recognizing in myself a growing mercilessness in relation to my brother and the younger cousins. Any chance we older children got, we terrorized them; now I was a participant terrorist. Although I was shocked by my behavior, I could not take the risk of losing my place with the group, nor did I want anything but to do to someone else what had been done to me. Being terrorized and terrorizing seems to be a chain reaction, which takes more strength to stop than I had then.

Eventually, too, I came to understand how my cousins had felt about me and my brother at first. Later, after I finally belonged, when a new person of any age came to the ranch, his or her presence felt like a splinter under my fingernail. This new person was to be gotten rid of. It was a combined feeling of lording it over the awkward newcomer and resenting the objectification of my life that seeing through his or her eyes meant to me. I could not remain in my oneness with nature when this stranger was noticing things.

As children, we had numerous unpleasant ways of making a newcomer feel unwelcome. Having experienced most of these myself, I could guess only too well how we were making this new person feel. But, instead of feeling empathic to other outsiders, I joined in with my cousins against them.

We treated adults more carefully than children because, of course, they could fight back. Mostly we were aloof and disdainful, but we also tended to show off in daring physical activities. Our tree climbing was more hazardous than usual, and we took more chances on horseback or in the ocean. I suppose most of this behavior was lost on the adults, but outsider children certainly noticed. With them, we not only extended ourselves in our physical tricks but seduced them into going along with us. If they refused, we would make them feel like sissies; there was no more devastating label.

We would swing hand over hand out on the rafters in the hay barn to drop many feet onto hard hay bales below. These landings hurt, but we would not let on, so that the visitors would feel bad if they indicated pain. Swimming way out beyond the breakers, racing horses bareback along the beach, climbing very high into pine trees, or leaping from boulder to boulder in the rock canyons—all these exploits, and many more, were intended to intimidate.

There was more than cruelty in our behavior; there was anxiety. I remember the huge roundup parties that were held when I was young, and I suppose the same problem must have existed as my mother experienced at her branding party. One roundup I remember happened after I had finally become an "insider." No one expected anything social of us children, so we were free to keep attuned to the cattle work and, when we were old enough, to participate in it. But I do remember being aware of the presence of others, all dressed up in "cowboy clothes" we would not have been seen dead in, smoking and drinking and so busy talking to each other that they might have been having a lawn party, except for the thick, flying dust and the noise of the men and cattle.

On one such occasion, I was along on the job of getting the beef for the barbecue. I think there were a couple of guest children along, too. A yearling heifer had been brought to the barn, and I remember the ranch hand taking a great sledge hammer, drawing it back like a baseball bat, and smashing the heifer right in the forehead with it. She fell like a stone, first to her knees and then to her chest, and then she tipped over. I, of course, did not let on my shock, but shocked I was. To this day, I can hear the terrible thunk of the hammer connecting with her skull.

Then she was strung up by her hind legs on two hooks, slit down the middle, degutted, and patiently skinned, small stroke after small stroke, with the sharp knife. The whole job, including cutting her up, took only a few hours; soon great chunks of beef were sizzling away on the great outdoor barbecue at one of my uncles' houses, up on the hill above the Big House.

After the ranch had been sold, when I returned there to choose property for my mother, I was technically the outsider. But I truly felt that all those women and men involved with the real estate development were really the outsiders. It was more than the fact that they were dressed somehow to look like ranchers; it had also to do with the way they were undertaking to convert our wild, free, open place into a fenced, diminished, sterilized setting, laced with roads. Roads were being forced up into canyons beyond the forbidding rock shelf that had always protected the back country high up on the ridge. Now you could get up there with a four-wheel-drive vehicle; worse, there was a road going all the length of that ridge, from one end to the other. The ranch was being tamed and cut to pieces.

Perhaps our subtle fear of outsiders had had to do with just what finally happened. Perhaps we children knew, unconsciously, that the ranch was in danger—that if enough outsiders knew what a wonder it was, they would find a way to take it from us. And we would not know how to stop them. Which is, of course, what finally happened.

Everyone knows that nature, including humans, can be ruthless, but we may not all agree on how to live with that fact. When, as a newcomer to the ranch, I first met with this ruthlessness in my cousins, I felt terribly shocked and afraid. But I did not experience it as wrong, somehow. They put me through frightening, painful, and humiliating experiences, and I hated it. But I knew I had no choice. Their behavior toward me was no worse and no better than their behavior toward my brother and toward other cousins who came to the ranch after us. Ruthless though it was, their behavior was impersonal; no personal offense was intended.

And it was not only my cousins; horses are nature, too. The Shetland ponies, for instance, were just as ruthless in their excellent efforts to get rid of us. The ponies were as impersonal about it as my cousins were; they treated everyone in the same way.

I remember another story of Shetland ruthlessness with a particular shudder because it involved Grandmother's saddle. She did not use it; after her first, disastrous ride, during which her horse ran away with her, she never rode again. But the saddle remained "Grandmother's saddle," and it was a humiliation for me in itself. It was flatter than regular cowboy saddles and padded, and it had no horn. I felt ridiculous on it, and the jokes made about it made everything worse.

One day my cousins and I were riding along and came to a wide stream too broad to jump. So my Shetland walked out into the middle of it and lay down. I kicked him madly as I felt his legs fold up under me, but it did no good. I got my feet out of the stirrups and jumped off just before he rolled in the water. I stood hopelessly by, in water up to my knees, watching that wretched pony roll back and forth over Grandmother's saddle.

What saved the saddle, finally, was the very thing I hated about it, its design. Being flat and soft and hornless, it suffered little damage. It was soggy and muddy but not broken.

When the others had gotten my pony to its feet, I had to crawl back up on that slippery saddle and begin the miserable trip home, to be greeted by grunts and criticisms from the men and another wave of humiliation.

In time I learned to keep my pony moving across streams by kicking and kicking, never letting him stop. In response, he would use another trick. As we got to the other side at a good speed, spraying water everywhere, he would clench his teeth onto the bit and go even faster. Soon he was running away, and I had lost control yet again.

The feeling of having to figure out everything for myself, with no help from people or nature, was pervasive. And so it was for everyone. We all had to go it alone. The only way to learn from someone else was by imitation. It was lonely and scary, but when I learned something it was really mine, and I could take credit for it. Each newly learned process added another bit of confidence, too, until I began to realize I had the means to learn whatever I needed to know.

The ruthlessness of ranch and wilderness life is neither good nor bad in itself; it is good or bad according to the individual's experience of it. Some people thrive; others are injured by it. The word "ruth" means "pity." So, "ruthlessness" means only "without pity." It does not really mean "cruel," though it is sometimes used that way. Years later, as I became aware of the personal dimension of life and of my feeling links to individuals rather than to collectives, I lost this hard-won neutral attitude of being "without pity." As an adult, I discovered empathy and felt pain when another person did. My behavior changed, as a result, and I could no longer watch impassively when nature took her ruthless course.

I remember my horror a few years ago as I saw a big snake swallowing a living frog, bit by bit. I heard strange sounds and realized that the frog was screaming. Its hind legs and lower body had already disappeared down the snake's throat. It's head and front legs (arms!) and the upper part of its body were still visible, and as it screamed it clawed the air and tried to lurch out of the snake's mouth. As I watched the visible part get smaller, I felt like pulling the frog out, but could not. I could not find a side to ally with; the snake needed to feed to stay alive just as the frog needed to escape to stay alive. If not this frog, then another frog. My old impersonal attitudes reawakened and I too became ruthless. But I was not able to stay and watch; I turned and left. I will never forget the screaming.

Without a ruthless attitude as a child I could never have held a red-hot branding iron to the soft, brown flank of a terrified calf. Even harder would have been those first few times, when I hesitated in my placing of the branding iron and burned the calf over a bigger area. Not only was the brand blurred; I hurt the calf more than was necessary. I doubt that I could brand a calf today.

Eventually I realized that, first as a child in the wilderness and then as an adult, I had learned "both sides"—ruthlessness and empathy—since I had also experienced human and animal caring. And I learned that it is necessary to be able to "hold the opposites," choosing between the two if I must, but never denying the value of the opposite. "Everything has its season," including ruthlessness, and sometimes its opposite, empathy, has to be set aside so as to get on with the job at hand. Doctors and nurses have to develop this attitude, for example, or they will increase pain unnecessarily.

There is an old ranch story of the time one of the men got drunk and his horse managed to carry him home safely by shifting under his weight when he seemed to be falling off. This horse resolutely held her path down the middle of the road, forcing the driver of a car to detour into the field in order to go around her.

Given the generally impersonal basis of life on the ranch, it is impressive to see an animal's capacity to take such responsibility for its human partner. This phenomenon is the "other side" of the ruthlessness an animal must be capable of if it is to survive. Again, both sides are part of the whole picture.

One day, when I was about ten, I rode with a younger cousin through my aunt's rose garden. She had always headed us off from doing so in the past, but on this day she was not in sight, so we did the forbidden thing. There was a sudden upheaval of my world, a crash and an explosion of dust, and I found myself at the bottom of a great pit. I was wedged against a corner post, sitting on the floor of this pit, and the thousand-pound horse I had been riding bareback was sitting in my lap. Like a dog on its haunches, he had his rump jammed against my legs, and I looked up his long back to his head, which was high in the air since he was propped up on his front legs. He was so big that he took up all the space in the pit, except for the tiny area I was occupying behind him. Suddenly I found myself flying up the slope of his back; I will never know how I managed it. My cousin reached her hand down to me and hauled. Then, just as suddenly, I was out and looking down on the great horse, sitting patiently down in the hole.

His name was Sueco, and he had been my grandfather's roping horse for years. His age and wisdom probably saved my life. He had made no move while I was beneath him, nor had he moved while I used his back as a ramp to the surface. Sueco stayed quiet until a derrick was brought in to lift him out. Like the drunk's mare, Sueco had responded to my plight with exactly what was needed. How fortunate for me that the no-longer-used septic tank had been empty in the first place—but even more, that animal wisdom is as much a reality as animal ruthlessness.

8

THE LAND

~ JANE ~

July, much more than any other time, reveals what the land basically looks like. One is not drawn off into imagination or feelings by luxurious color. There is only what lies right there before you. In order to choose property with an eye to owning it, July is the acid test.

It had been my idea that rather than sell all the ranches in one fell swoop, we might perhaps be able to divide the coast ranch into thousand-acre lots for the members of the family. Of course, this was a pipe dream, because we already knew that a corporation could not give away or sell pieces of land without listing these divisions as income to the corporation and being subject to large income taxes.

But at least I wanted to play with the idea, and I hoped beyond hope that such a move might work. Also, the wishful thinking gave me the impetus to drive the whole length of the coast ranch mesas and test them from the viewpoint of individual ownership. Chaparral covered the rough back country at that time, making it inaccessible by car and much too difficult to evaluate.

When I returned for my July trip, the spring flower population, like everything else in summer, had ended. Only a few inconspicuous summer varieties survived in the creek beds. Here and there, bunches of white blossoms on the toyon shrubs forecast our indigenous Christ-mas holly. Goldenrod brightly spread golden blossoms in long sprays clothing the dry hillsides. More than the remembered green of spring, these small, intense spots of color loudly spoke for themselves against the eternal tans and browns.

Heading by car toward El Cojo, our westernmost boundary, I was confronted, at the Llegua and Gato mesas, with a strange phenomenon. Out there, stretching into the distance, were vast fields of standing, dry volunteer hay, a combination of mustard and wild oats. The hay was so dry it could have burst into flame without warning. The vegetation was alive with hot potential, waiting for some dreadful calamity: someone's careless match or a spark from the locomotive on the nearby railroad tracks. Acres and acres of mesa, brittle and hot and in intolerable tension, were on the ready. The red of the mustard stalks only added to the frightening effect. The vast, shining fields, polished and burnished as though by friction, were screaming out the impending danger. Loki was poised for his wild, crackling dance. There was, besides, the ever-ready wind in the offing to spread the disaster, should it happen. Memories of weeks of brushfires brought back old spasms of panic. One spark would be enough.

Leo, spread out on the hills overlooking the mesas, was about to add his bit. In the wings, he could have been luxuriating over the vulner-able, ungrazed range: the hills, as dry as the fields below, were actually taking on the look of a lion's tawny hide. Their anatomy showed just enough to clinch the comparison. It was easy to see how the concept had originated and why in this country the sun that Leo symbolizes was, for us as well as for the Chumash, destructive. Yet the threat of fire was no worse than what would happen if anonymous, uncaring populations spread like a plague over the ranch's acres.

Paradoxically, the old magic came back with my concern, and the familiar landmarks touched on still deeper layers of memory. But one cannot dwell too long on potential disaster. One has to be fatalistic in July, when the coast is in its most vulnerable state. The Chumash called July "month when everything blows away" (*hesiqʔ momoyʔ an ciwolhoyoyo*). We might have named July "month when everything shrivels in the heat." August, heralding the end of summer, is not so threatening.

The coast was indeed at its worst that July, but to relieve it there were the ever-present friendly, beckoning little places, the trees, the birds, and, on that day, the soft, mildly relaxed ocean automatically pushing into its returning tide.

The coast in July maintains character mostly because of its rock strata and the shrubs and the small wild things softening them. It is no mean achievement at the hottest, lowest ebbtime of the year. But then, in old age, so are thoughts of death, like immense rock formations, softened by the personal concerns of those who care.

Parking the car on the bluff overlooking El Cojo's beach, I strolled down to see what was going on down there. Many gulls were resting; numerous white, round splashes with dark centers dotting the wet sand were their droppings. So many was evidence that the gulls had been content to stay in one place most of that mild day. When I appeared, they jawed at each other and strode about as though to push for some concerted action. There were old-timers among them, and a few small black ones. Other, gray ones, no bigger, predominated and were conspicuous for their white heads and red bills.

A man's intercom voice broke in, loud and clear and persistent and low on the water. The drilling ship next to the Phillips platform, where the voice had originated, was probably at least three miles away. But the voice seemed to materialize at my elbow, from out of nowhere: a lunatic voice calling. Fortunately, once I went around the headland, it was shut off.

A large gull glided slowly up the beach overhead—clean and clear and white against an azure sky—its wings tipped in black, its rosy feet tucked up under its tail, and its red bill showing clearly against the blue.

The buff cliffs were slightly pink that day. Within them are the remains of prehistoric elephants, a botanist had once told me. Remains of the Pleistocene era are in the upper strata of the ocean cliffs, he had said. I was reminded of a rainy winter day when, as a child, I had walked the tracks with my father—the road having been washed out—to the San Augustine flag station. Three miles west of the house, in the last railroad cut, we saw a mammoth's tusk embedded in the bank. By its girth it must have been at least six feet long. The rains eroding the banks had uncovered it. Later, we dug it out of its ancient wash, and I felt a certain first importance when I was given the honor of donating it to the local museum of natural history, where it is now. I was only twelve and home from boarding school for my first Christmas vacation without my twin. He was away at an Eastern school, so I could usurp one of the few chances to be important. A memory like that was bound to stick.

On this July day, I watched how the ocean at noon was muddy blue at one moment, then a deep, clear blue, and then, to the south, believe it or not, a lovely, soft light blue. I could not account for such kaleidoscopic changes.

The cove at El Cojo, for us the most remote, lonely place of our past, was filled with barges and boats. Not far beyond loomed the oil platform, its dredging barge and drilling boat near it. The charm of this lonely spot had gone. One might as well be on the San Francisco waterfront, where such a conglomeration can be the city's biggest attraction. Harbor life can appeal to the artists and poets and nostalgic sea-loving people. Not here in Little Cojo. Man-made traffic only neutralized it into nothing.

Long ago, in my childhood, a fisherman had lived here alone. The ocean had been in his watering, light blue eyes and bent figure. He would give us fish from time to time, as rent for his driftwood shack. The contribution had been a guarantee against his possibly declaring squatter's rights, one of the hazards of the early days. Money had hardly counted then; barter was the usual medium of exchange, and my father was always a gracious host, no matter how humble his guest. The fisherman—old Perry, we called him—suddenly disappeared while we were still little. A mysterious cloud hung over his going. Most likely he had been found dead in his lean-to and packed out on a horse for the county coroner to deal with. In those days no one talked about death, so we never knew. His makeshift cabin was, for us, always haunted—a place to be leery of. We would have done better with the truth. Death of one's own kind was somehow shameful, at best a mystery, but not unknown on the ranch. Bodies washed ashore from time to time: fishermen who had drowned when their small boats were blown out to sea by offshore gales.

It was quiet at El Cojo; yet even the sight of the boats and barges, symbolizing noise, spoiled its serenity for me. No thin, wild trails led onto the beach. The imprints of tiny feet and the big pawprints of predators following them were not there to tell a story. They had been driven out.

The intimate, isolated quiet, ordinarily teeming with an undercurrent of life, was gone from El Cojo. The wild magic we had known as children had dispersed—withdrawn like the sea anemone, which knows before you touch it.

Tepitates, the highest place on the ridge back of the cove, was dramatic to look at. In the language of the Chumash, Tepitates meant "A Sacred High Place." I could see it from where I stood, next to the car. It was grand and impersonal, and the creek streaming from it was full. The mesas below were the broadest of all, with expanses of flatland for building. The range on the foreground hills was good for cattle. The flats were fertile, but they would have to be shared with a neighbor. Vandenberg Air Force Base was only a few crow miles to the north (there was only one way to measure distance when the missiles were zooming overhead). I did not know then that one day a road would be built to Tepitates, making it accessible, and I would make my home there. In the past, being more in tune with the mesas, I had overlooked it.

Faint signs of the previous month's pastels still showed. The black-green oaks grew blacker than ever against the tawny fur of the undergrazed hills. There was a bumper range crop; the cattle could not keep up with it. This country was what the Yankees with money in their eyes had first encountered.

From there, Point Conception was like a medieval castle on the horizon; the light in its tower and its bastions made it so. Seen from close up, when our parents went there by horse and cart along the beach to vote and we, the twins, went on foot rather than be cooped up, it had been overall a small affair. Only the revolving light had seemed, on its stump of a tower, immense and filled with purpose.

Now, soft, tan-gray doves were everywhere, their stubby, pink feet showing in the gray dust alongside the road. Small larks, with their black velvet horned caps, flipped up and down the dusty road in bursts of flight to keep ahead of my car. Acres and acres of dusty weeds were brightened a little by insignificant yellow flowering plants: tar weeds, which are ruinous to crops. Scattered oat fields high up on the hilltops turned into anonymous white patches. A barely green undercoat of the range in the Barranco Hondo Creek area intensified two small hill peaks. The dry, clean dust was suffocating. An abandoned exploration oil rig on Gato Mesa reminded me of a long-gone feeling: we would someday be rich. Luckily, that day had never come! I could never have withstood the unreality of wealth.

Magic is not to be owned or imprisoned or trapped or domesticated or improved upon. By its nature, it is fleeting and momentary, in the offing, forever returning but never staying. Primitives called it "mana." It touches only those who are thin skinned. Those who know the magic's fleeting nature are doomed by the need forever to seek, because their human centers also are tied to the fleeting, unscheduled unexpectedness. Others, less aware but equally sensitive, are crippled for life when "it," the magic, is taken from them, because the wild center in which the human center unknowingly lodges is no longer "theirs."

Ownership, under the best conditions, somehow could not promote those stolen moments that reveal the unexpected. Meaning will not be owned. Ownership could never foster those times that are just so. The Other will not be possessed; it has a life of its own. Strange how ownership of the ranch had never, until that visit, become an issue for me. I did not remember ever having had the sense of owning our properties. In fact, this day's attempt to visualize ownership in general were beginning to drive away the point of being there at all! My own experience was getting in the way of my enjoyment.

Gato Canyon, back of the mesas, was inviting. It reached high up to Tepitates. Its foreground flats were rich and protected, and the hills were interesting. Barranco Hondo Creek swerved close to Gato Creek there, providing a fine alluvial delta, which is excellent cropland. This could have been *the* place for some gentleman farmer.

The area framed by the Llegua and Chiclan creeks seemed barren viewed from the small holding corrals, its only protected spot. The road dust was forbidding, although the many thriving oaks indicated underground water. The San Augustine was by far the most attractive canyon of this area. It was easy to see why it had been the home base of our renters, C.H. and O.B. Fuller, installed after my grandfather died and my grandmother was in charge (pioneers had a nose for the best places); their presence accounted for the large eucalyptus grove. Three varieties grew there. Threatened by loss as I was that day in 1962, I realized I had never really seen this canyon. Like an animal, I had been caught in my territorial rituals, defending my land with all my wit and nerve but never really looking at it. Yet, trip after trip, I recognized every stone in the trail, every odd formation, every old oak. Memories of detail belong to childhood, when, being small, one is also in detail.

In the San Augustine, an appealing small complex of pointed hills filled up a wide space between the western ridge of the Chiclan and the eastern ridge of the Pescado. Three creeks, the Chiclan, the San Augustine, and the Pescado, came together there, forming between them a happy open place in the midst of the summer season's browns. The flats below the hills were perhaps the richest land on the whole coast. There was also an abundance of water, thanks to my geologist brother, Joe, who had drilled horizontal wells in the rock wall strata high up at the canyon's source. The view down the flats toward the ocean was pleasing; during winter storms, white sprays from the breakers showed above the tracks. It might be possible someday, once Texaco was through with its depradations, to live in such a place and feel contained. Spirits of the Chumash, who are known to have made that canyon their home, might have given it quality. It is hard not to think so. The Santa Anita, the site of the original adobe headquarters, was no longer inviting. Why, why, why did Grandfather, loving the land as he did, let "them" put the railroad clear across every lovely ocean view for these twenty-five miles? Perhaps, like a father with too many children, he could not think out the destiny of all his acres. He was, besides, caught by the concept of "progress." Progress that moved onward and upward, always in a vertical direction, until it died of lost energy, an energy that had never turned back on itself for renewal and depth. The cyclical, spiral sense of progress of the Indian would never have allowed such desecrations!

The Sacate and La Cuarta were also snubbed off by the tracks: it became clear why the San Augustine and the Bulito were exceptions! Extensive foreground land had saved them from Grandfather's progressiveness. But I had never minded the trains routinely rattling by at night. I had rather liked the feeling that the trains scheduled us a bit and gave us the tenuous connection with structured civilization that we needed. Each time a train passed, the old house shook. It gave me a feeling of living in a toy house, a feeling that fit the grandeur of the country. Nevertheless, I still felt an old first-comer's sense of superiority when I watched passengers, propped up and framed in the train windows, jangling through our wild space, staring before them at nothing!

That evening the superintendent talked about Agua Caliente Canyon, a place I hardly knew. It lay at the easternmost end of our coast ranch, close to California's Highway 101, making it vulnerable to beach-hungry populations. Approaching it early the next morning, I was relieved to find that it was nothing to look at from the road. It need not be a target for the greedy. Inside, in the still, watery sunlight, it lay in absolute silence. Bird life there so early in the morning was slow to stir. Steep, rounded hills, tanned and softened by the mustard and brought to life in the slight wind, tapered off at the beach cliffs. They guarded both sides of the canyon and hid, by means of the narrow entrance, the canyon's extensiveness.

Belonging created an insensitivity to the spirit of the place. And, as I had already begun to suspect, collective ownership like ours might be its death. On the other hand, I might have been speaking with the language of old age. My own life was that involved. Personal needs, interwoven as they were with the larger situation, were perhaps only echoes of the fate of that beautiful coast. Ownership and death, identification and death, *are* connected. There was, indeed, a need to continue with the notes. I was not through yet!

On the way to the Agua Caliente, I had noticed for the first time that Sacate Creek flowed into the middle of the large beach crescent made up of Coyote Canyon to its west and La Cuarta Canyon to its east. Farther along, in the Agua Caliente area, there was no extensive beach property, nor access points by beach to attract the hordes. And the wind kicked up an awful row there.

Already, in early morning, the Agua Caliente's entire western ridge above the first narrows was in full sunlight. Some seepage, a spillover from big springs a mile or so above, showed up on the opposite ridge. In that area, water traveled through faults and cracks farther than one would think. In fact, one of the ranch's four faults, named after this canyon, was marked by a jumble of strata, suggesting that there had been some catastrophic movement of the mountain range. The viaduct for the railroad tracks across the Agua Caliente's mouth was out of sight here. The oaks were not showing the effects of drought, as they did over most of the ranch.

With no warning, my car sank ignominiously, hopelessly, into a bog in the road. I had not seen it. The mishap gave me an excuse to abandon the car and see the canyon in more detail, on foot.

The narrows at the first rock ledge were not narrow at all, as they were elsewhere. The canyon spread out in all directions, as though it had been wrenched, yanked, dispersed by unseen, impersonal forces. The brush and trees had filtered into the cozy places left by moving slabs of rock.

I walked down the broad road under grove after grove after grove of oaks, feeling as if the canyon would never end. Huge oaks, interlacing high over my head, their handsome trunks like twisted, great pillars of strength, ensured the silence and intimacy. The sun, by then glaring, lit up the other side of the creek. It made the rocks and leaves and ledges there stand out in contrast to the cool, black shade on my side. There was not a sound, not the slightest wind. Only once did the gently graded road make a violent twist down and up again across a side canyon. Never have there been so many oaks massed together! The fog had piled up over the Gaviota Canyon, but it lacked the push to penetrate to where I was. Its ragged edge in the distance barely showed over the hill.

Abutting Highway 1, at the extreme northern end of the Agua Caliente, was a quiet valley. The broad flare of this fan-shaped meadow measured at least a mile on our border, or so Pacheco, our horse breaker, had told me. He should know, because in my father's old age it had been Pacheco's job to keep track of the range. Summer flowers survived there in the cool shade of the oaks, and elderberry trees were burdened by large, hanging bunches of ripe, blue berries. Flooding sunshine supported succulents, deer vetch, morning glory, and sprays of a small variety of orange-red flower growing on the creek bank. It was the fantastic beauty that let you come to yourself. Harmony is, after all, the principal ingredient of objective beauty.

In Agua Caliente Canyon, I was as though swimming in the limitless ocean, unhampered, the wild elements against my skin, with no fear of being disturbed—or even of being seen. Thousands of tiny wild paw tracks, large ones among them, were recorded in the fine gray dust: an abundance of unseen life caressing the atmosphere with quizzical noses and bright eyes. The creatures apparently had had no fear of being spied upon, for they had walked boldly down the middle of the road. Tracks of mice, rats, squirrels, kangaroo rats, skunks, coyotes, foxes, and deer were crisscrossed by those of the birds and, occasionally, by the wavy line of a snake. With luck, but rarely, I spotted the enormous pugmark of a puma. There were no signs of the raccoons, because they followed the creeks. Man, a rare visitor here, was no threat to the wild creatures, and I was under orders to be respectful during my own small invasion of their habitat. It was paradoxical that the canyon closest to civilization, unlike our most isolated places at the western end, was the most inhabited by wild creatures.

Several oaks, as huge as any I had ever seen, and not particularly gnarled, were there. The wind did not drive into that place much. Moss hung in the oaks at the first major fork, more of it on the western creek bank, indicating moisture, and fog, in the air. The Agua Caliente did not funnel the wind out of the north to the sea as did the canyons at the western end of the ranch.

It was a brisk hour's walk from my bogged-down car to the main ranch road. Under the viaduct, beside the beach where I had hoped to flag a passerby to help me with my car, I saw a killdeer flying in wide circles. It was yelling as though the devil were after it. Indeed, it was the devil himself: a ruby-red hummingbird! He dive-bombed the killdeer mercilessly until he finally drove it away. A strange battle; although it was late in the year, it must have involved a nest. At low tide, the breakers were still nearly reaching the breakwater.

9

OWNERSHIP AND DEFINITION

OF THE SELF

~ *LYNDA* ~

My mother and I started out with the same problem in working out our loss of the ranch, and that was the problem of ownership. She says the ranch was not the ranch when she thought about owning a piece of it, which was one idea being considered at the time of liquidation. My view is that the ranch owned us, and that is why it would not have solved the problem of loss to buy back even a big piece of it. To me, losing the land meant losing the way I identified myself. I was being cast out of the land, not by the land itself but by human reality. It was practical, economically necessary, inevitable, that we go away from there. The land was not rejecting us, which made the leaving even harder. We had to rip ourselves out of the womb of it; our civilized world demanded it.

What I lost was a feeling of being undefined, of being relaxed into myself. I could assume my truest form—a fluidity—on the ranch. That had been one of the hardest parts of finding my way into the ranch as a child, discovering this way of being that ultimately worked so well for me. Before moving to the ranch at age seven, I had learned techniques and postures that were expected in city life. I had learned a certain set of manners that adapted me to society. On the ranch, these manners and techniques separated me from the others—in fact, they separated me from my truest self.

Psychologists talk about the ego and the Self. The ego has to do with the conduct of one's daily life as it moves from birth to maturity to death. The Self, on the other hand, has to do with one's link to life as it continues, transcending these daily issues.

An inadequate analogy to the Self has been suggested: electricity exists as a potential whether it manifests or not. The manifestations (e.g., light bulbs, lightning) are as finite as we individuals are. But the phenomenon is limitless. Thus, the analogy goes, we, in our egos and finite lives, are manifestations of the Self and of infinite life.

The ranch was a manifestation of the wilderness. For me, the wilderness is an image that is greater than the world. For me, the world is limited because it is a definable fact, and wilderness is not. The ranch, before selling became a consideration, was wilderness greater than the world. From this recognition of the paradoxical difference between "world" and "wilderness" I have come to understand that the world carries the meaning of "ego" for me, while the ranch, as I knew it when it was still wild, meant "Self." In her exploration of the ranch, my mother came to think that the wilderness mirrors the Self.

As I have contemplated this idea of my mother's, I have come to understand that there is an apparently contradictory combination of qualities offered by the wilderness that makes it so apt as a mirror of the Self. One is the way the wilderness can be felt as a container and a safe place; the other is the way it feels unboundaried and scary. I think the containment comes from knowing it is bigger and stronger than I am; it is analogous to the feeling I had as a child about my parents and other adults. They could take care of me. Because we were not supervised on the ranch I transferred this feeling from humans to the ranch itself, as my mother had before me. The ranch became the source of power and nourishment and fear. Even though I did not know how big the ranch was, I felt it was big enough, and that was the main requirement to feel contained by it. A container does not have to be finite; in fact, it is more enhancing to growth if it is infinite. It does, however, need to be embracing and familiar in some way. Because I grew up in the dry, windy coastal region of California I find that climate and terrain familiar, wherever it may be. The countryside in Greece feels like home, as it does in Kenya; the northeastern Atlantic coast feels familiar, as does the high terrain in Utah's Uinta Mountains, where I go horse-packing. On the other hand, the Hindu Kush area, with its barren slopes and shocking peaks in the northwestern Himalayas of Pakistan, felt utterly alien and terrifying to me and thus had to do with the terrifying aspect of the Self. The more modest environs of Kathmandu seemed far friendlier.

The unboundaried aspect of the wilderness permits us to stretch to our fullest dimensions. Moving through it provides experiences of superseding presumed limitations of courage, stamina, and strength. We find we are doing more than we thought we could, in a variety of ways. It seems as if the very environment buoys us up even as its challenges threaten to defeat us. I remember times on horseback, when I was still new to the ways of horses, being so scared at the prospect of descending a steep cliff or jumping a roaring creek that I would feel numb. The horse, an old hand at such things, would simply take charge and go where he had to go in order to keep up with the others. I would be thrown around in the saddle, hanging on to the horn.

But each time, I came through with no more than a few cuts and bruises. Usually I stayed in the saddle, but even when I fell off I suffered no harm, really.

It is the nature of living things to seek the unexplored. It has been shown in studies on rats that the drive to explore is as strong in them as the drives for food, water, and sex. Exploration has been the hallmark of human ambition. A challenge may scare us to death, but it also fuels inspiration and vigor, and life may slow down too much without it. I feel that this sort of "death" (caused by fear) can result in the emergence of something new: a new attitude, a new understanding, a new way of living. Challenge, too, connects us with the Self.

Finding my way into the ranch and finding my way into my truest self coincided, aiding and abetting each other. The more I was my most natural, the more welcome I felt in nature. I became part of nature, discovering both my capacity to hear and feel nature as it goes about its business and my capacity to hear and feel my own systems of breathing, sweating, cooling, hunger, and itching as I moved through grass, dust, shade, and water. This process, as I discussed earlier, is one way to find the Self, and in this way I am contained by the Self; I am merged in the Self; I am owned by the Self. It is in this sense that I believe my mother and I are owned by the ranch.

When the idea arose of family members each choosing a thousand acres or so to own personally, my mother found that she could not seriously consider it. For her, owning one section of the ranch would have reversed the fact of who owns whom. She would then have been the owner of a thousand acres, well surveyed, with properly defined boundaries. Again, owning land was not the meaning of the ranch for either of us, because it would have destroyed the feeling of limitlessness we had both grown up with.

Paradoxically, when my mother was offered the small parcel of her choice, years after the ranch had been sold as an agricultural commune, the feeling was right. I think this may have been because she was buying only a hundred acres. Thus, she was buying a spot: a center to sit in, high up in one corner of the ranch, from where she could see in all directions. The ranch was still there, spreading away from her spot and visually accessible. Boundaries did not matter, since there were no fences; she could merge with all she saw: ridge, canyons, hills, mesas, beach, and ocean. Had she bought a thousand-acre canyon, she would have felt limited by the "canyon" definition and by responsibility for fences, land management, roads, and, perhaps, stock. In her relatively tiny parcel, there is no management needed beyond that having to do with the house and its systems. Her property line is somewhere down the slope of the canyon, but it does not particularly matter where. The only stock she has is wild—foxes, rabbits, snakes, mountain lions—and they do not worry about the unfenced boundaries. So my mother can again feel contained in the Self, with all the sense of being most natural that that permits.

I wonder what my great-grandfather—my mother's paternal grandfather—felt about the ranch. He accumulated the properties in the 1860s and 1870s, at a time when California land had relatively little value. He also lost properties, or sold them, in a way his son, my grandfather, never did. Great-grandfather may have felt that he owned the land, since he had bought it. But I would guess that my grandfather was owned by the land, since he was born on it. Certainly, my grandfather had been adamant about holding the ranch intact and, in fact, about acquiring more land. As my mother says, there was no possibility of liquidating the properties until after his death.

Both my mother and I were born into the ranch psychologically, even though we were born elsewhere literally. As soon as each of us came there as a child, in our different eras, we felt enveloped by it. Again, the ranch owned us.

I wonder if one could say that buying land may preclude being owned by it, in fact, may preclude its representing the experience of the Self. The buying of land is a contradiction to the infinity of nature and the Self. You cannot buy nature or the Self. Buying land means creating finite borders. A window out is necessary if the Self is to be experienced. Such a window is possible if a bought property is adjacent to the wilderness, or to the ocean or desert. But a bought property surrounded by other bought properties may really be more of a daily life experience, a place to rest and gather together in a civilized way. It is a place to be sheltered from society; yet, by definition, being surrounded by other bought properties means that other people are around—the family within, neighbors around the perimeter. Man-made sounds, communication, and activity predominate over the sounds of nature.

Since we are a social species, I believe in such settings, but I also believe we will shrivel up as individuals if we have no opportunity to merge with the Self and the sense of infinity given us by the wilderness.

If one of the reasons that the ranch held us so well—owned us—was the fact that we second, third, and fourth generations were born into it, then another reason might be that we did not know where its boundaries were. Perhaps it was part of the ranch myth, but the fact is that no one in the family ever seemed to know just how big the property was. Even when it was sold, I never heard a definite figure for its acreage. I think this may have been an unconscious way to protect its mystique and its power to represent the Self. The Self cannot be defined, drawn, captured in any way; that is the whole point of the concept. We can be captured by the Self, however, and there is a real danger in that, as my mother and I experienced when we realized we were losing the ranch. If the manifestation of the Self dies, whether it be land, a powerful parent, a career, or some other form, the individual contained in it can die too. It takes a strong mobilization of consciousness, thought, feeling, and support to withstand the tendency to follow into a form of death, literal or figurative. My mother's careful exploration of the ranch and complete recording of her experience was such a mobilization. She had to swim with great determination out of her unconscious identification, her state of oneness, with the ranch and into an awareness of its value for her. Because of that work, she can now afford to merge with the ranch from her spot, her vantage point, her small parcel within it. She can both identify and disidentify with the infinity.

A third way in which the ranch carried the feeling of infinity for me, besides through its wildness and lack of boundaries, was the result of its lying along the coast. Standing with my back to the land, I could look out to sea forever. I felt the Pacific Ocean to be limitless. Sometimes I could see the Channel Islands, thirty miles out, but they provided no barrier to the sense of freedom and expansiveness the ocean conveyed.

It seems to me that owning land is not the best way to merge with nature and the Self. Far more valuable are the great wilderness areas of the world. Such places provide the same feeling I had as a child in the untouched space of the ranch. The spirit can expand forever in a place without fences, roads, or people. Since it is no longer feasible to hand great properties down through the generations, and since there are fewer and fewer undeveloped land areas in temperate zones into which we can expand, the urge to explore has had to be directed into other realms altogether. Such realms include space, ocean depths, and the smaller-than-small areas of physical science.

But the great wilderness areas still exist. Even if we have no inclination to go there, perhaps we can feel the expansion of spirit that comes with knowing that the wilderness exists and letting our imaginations carry us there.

10

THE BURN

~ JANE ~

Sometimes it becomes easier to give up a loved land when it has been spoiled. I remember a day in October 1962, when I went to the ranch to relive some of my nostalgic memories of the privacy and space and silence, and found, to my chagrin, that other plans had been made for me.

The superintendent announced on my arrival that we must have a look at the "controlled burn." He was proud of its success, and I must acknowledge it. Because of the burn, he said, the range would carry twice as many cattle! My reaction, kept to myself, of course, was less practical. Tampering with ten thousand acres of beautiful canyons, acres and acres covered with ceanothus that would otherwise be ridge-to-ridge deep blue in spring, seemed to be an insult, a degradation. I could not tell him that. And yet it was well known that the Indians had burned their land to increase feed for game. A sneaky thought surfaced: Such a desecration just might relieve me of my nostalgia for the place.

The burn had raked across more than ten miles of coastline. It had rubbed out the telling details that gave the land its character. The country had become anonymous, a land that could belong to anyone or everyone. The coastal substrata, nevertheless, showed up clearer than before. But somehow the arbitrary movements of the controlled burn had eliminated what originally had been opposing and balanced. A wildfire would have kept to its own natural laws of destruction. The prevailing wind would have driven it steadily in a certain direction, letting it die out in interesting places and skip over others.

This controlled, scientifically managed, calculated burn had swept the country clean. Wherever the guided fire had been reluctant to do its job, it had been relit, sometimes a number of times. When it had wanted to run wild it had been arbitrarily, rationally controlled by backfires. At dangerous points, firebreaks had been bulldozed. I felt as though a fine charcoal drawing, laid out before me, had not been given time for the fixing fluid to set before some giant hand had deliberately smudged it.

A mixture of feelings ensued: relief at not caring anymore and of being, for the time, cured of the place. Feelings of anger that the land's aboriginal character, known to the Chumash, was now gone for good. And a third reaction, the economic one: because of the elimination of sage and chaparral, the cattle herd would be increased. More cattle, more profit, could slow down the need to liquidate.

Preservation, they say, is a female concern—a feminine weakness. But preservation for whom? For people unconscious of the land's real meaning, who would never sense the importance of the wild? Or for people like the superintendent, who, without the wherewithal to own and love the smallest part of the ranch remained concerned with expediting his job? There were also those, like some of my family, who were unthinkingly in love with the land, if not unknowingly caught by the need to hang on for the sake of prestige. There were always those, besides, who, for the sake of security, animal-like, instinctively, defended their homeland.

The land's ever-returning, cyclic genius, especially if it is one's place of origin, also stirs thoughts of personal death and rebirth. It corrects our Western tendency to move ever "onward and upward" in a linear progression, working so hard for "more" and "better." Nature ultimately has the last word on such a narrow perspective, centering instead on the great round of life with its ever-new repetitions: new life emerging, maturing, dying, and emerging once again.

~ LYNDA ~

A fire is wonderful and terrible. But the effects of fire are only terrible. Perhaps an agriculturalist can see a planned burn as expanded-grazing-land-to-be, but a rancher is likely to see only the damage. The blackness is like too many crows, ominous and deathly, and the death is as if from bombing rather than accident.

My mother told me about the burn after it had been done, and it made me feel sad to hear about it. I was glad I would not have to see it. It sounded so abnormal—a scorched earth, an eradication. A so-called controlled burn leaves nothing. When the rains come, the seed that has been sown will sprout, and soon the blackness is softened by the new green. But the rancher remembers how it was, and the new scene is different. The normal variation in growth, from short to tall, sparse to lush, is gone. The differences in angle, foliage, color, stalkiness, round-ness, and height have all been burned away. What remains is homoge-neous. All the green is of the same height and more or less the same color. What is there, instead of the variety that nature prefers, is a man-made uniformity. It is soothing and dull and somehow false looking, like a park. The rancher will go there only as necessary to judge its readiness for cattle to be turned onto it.

My mother experienced both loss and a surcease from loss when she saw the wrecked land after the burn. There is less to lose if what you have is ruined. People will sometimes fight before a separation to reduce the value of the relationship that is going to be lost. Similarly, finding something that devalues the land can ease the prospect of leaving it.

Some years after my husband and I acquired a weekend place in Placerville, California, in the Sierra Nevada foothills, there was a wildfire in the area. We were not there when it happened; when we drove up the following weekend, expecting to find our place burned down, we drove through acres and acres of charred sticks, some as much as fifty feet tall. They were the remains of an extensive ponderosa pine forest that we had always taken for granted. Vast areas had the dead aspect of a war zone. But, as my mother noted, a wildfire does leave places unburned. Among the corpses of trees were patches of untouched sage and manzanita, and the red earth of that area known as the gold country was still red.

The feeling of loss remained with us, of course, even after we discovered that a firebreak had been bulldozed around our house, saving it. But there was also the awareness that spots of life continued all around us and might one day spread into the dead areas. Still, the gold country fire left us permanently disoriented. Even though we did not end up with homogeneity, it was clear that our place would never be the same. Friends said, "Oh, you won't notice the difference after the rains come and everything becomes green again." I tried, and failed, to explain that the loss of the trees and the feeling of forest was permanent. It could take a hundred years for the ponderosa to return; certainly we would never see it. Possibly it would not return at all. Eventually, another kind of tree might take over, or the manzanita might get so thick that trees would be unable to survive to maturity. We would always see the difference.

The fact of the wildfire in our Sierra foothill region made our subsequent moving away from there much easier. We were saddened by the loss of the forest, but we were also forced to become conscious, before we left, of what we had had there. The destruction of our forest in the gold country jolted us into the awareness that we had loved it.

After the fire, I spent a lot of time exploring undamaged forestland near our place that stretched away into a national forest, making a conscious connection and farewell to it. By the time we left, six years later, the hardest part had been done; the all-pervasive ache of loss had been reduced.

I am sure that my not having made a careful farewell to the ranch when it was sold twenty years earlier gave leaving the place in the Sierra foothills double meaning for me. Just as my mother was grateful for the partial relief of pain she experienced in seeing the controlled burn, I was half-aware that the wildfire in the mountains was a preliminary step in my freeing myself from entanglement with the land, all land. I think I will never again be so immersed in my environment that I will forget that I could lose it at any time. I feel this way, too, about the still-existing wildernesses around the world with which I have no personal connection. The specter of loss hovers like a crow. The crow is everywhere. The wilderness can no longer be taken for granted.

Although the aftermath of a fire is terrible, I find a fire in progress to be compelling. The roar and sweep of flames make me feel anxious and awed. My human powers of control feel diminished, and the authority of nature demands my respect. While I am afraid and hesitant, I am at the same time excited and attracted. Nature, again, activates the Self.

My first conscious experience of wildfire happened about a year or so after I had come to live on the ranch. We were going about our ranch-kid business at the barn one day when we became increasingly aware of heightened activity. The phone in the barn kept ringing, and the various ring combinations, long and short, indicated that everyone on the ranch was being contacted. Pickup trucks and station wagons began converging on the barn, and men jumped out to talk to each other. We finally understood that there was a fire. It had started in the western part of the ranch and was coming toward us in the home canyon. I had a picture in my mind of a huge wall of flame advancing across the mesas and canyons, like a burning tidal wave, coming to get us.

Somehow, we children found ourselves sitting in the back of a pickup pounding along toward the fire. The tailgate had been dropped, so our legs hung over the rear bumper. Two of us held on to the sides of the truck, but the other two, in the middle, had nothing to hang on to. I was one of those in the middle, and I was afraid I would be bounced off as the truck sped over the bumpy ranch road. Dust rolled up from the wheels and enveloped us; I doubt that the man driving the pickup would have noticed if one of us had fallen off.

Three canyons west of the barn, the truck turned off the road. We bumped over the field leading up to the low slope of hill where the firefighters were working with shovels, fire extinguishers, and bulldozers, trying to make a firebreak. The flames crawled toward us, low and erratic, the light wind pushing them along. There was no tidal wave of flame, but there was a sense that the fire was inexorable. Flames would seem to be extinguished, then jump into life again. The charred areas expanded, smoke still rising where there were no longer any flames. The gray ash blew in the wind and reignited as it fell on dry, unburned grass.

The men shouted and sweated and swung their shovels and pick-axes. The driver of our pickup jammed on the brakes some distance from the flames and jumped out. He pulled a shovel from the truck bed and shouted at us to bring along the cases of beer, which we had not noticed there.

We felt the excitement in the air and became excited ourselves. We hauled the cases of beer out of the truck and staggered up the slope with them. The heat and dust and fevered activity added to our sense of imminent disaster. Someone shouted that two thousand acres had already burned and that the fire line was a mile wide and the wind increasing. We were scared and exhilarated both; the whole scene was wild.

We dropped the beer by a rock where some fire equipment lay. Then, not knowing what to do, we opened a couple of beer cans with a can-opener attachment on someone's pocketknife. The beer was fizzy and squirted over us; it had been in the sun for a while and had been shaken up in the truck. It was bitter and warm, but we hardly noticed. The excitement of the fire had changed everything. None of us had had beer before, yet we drank it down. Its effect on us was immediate. Together with the heat of midday and the increasing smoke and dust, the beer transformed us into dervishes. We shouted and laughed and became one with the extraordinary energies stirred up by the fire.

The fire was finally contained hours later, after consuming three or four thousand acres. I have no memory of what we children did all afternoon or how we got home. I do know that I hate to drink beer in the sun; the scenes from that day come to my mind's eye if even the possibility of a beer on a hot day arises. I have a vague recollection of being headachy and nauseated; I wonder how much beer we drank.

I associate fire and frenzy; to this day, I feel anxious when there is danger of wildfire. It is the fear of fire, rather than the possibility of a water shortage, that disturbs me when there is a drought. And I know that the worry has everything to do with feeling, once again, that nature owns me and can wipe out my small power. Once again, the ego, the individual, must pay its respects to the overarching command of the Self and of nature, which mirrors it.

My mother discusses the tyranny of drought and how we were never prepared for it. I remember the "wet years," when Grandfather would run seven thousand head of cattle on the ranch. (And I will never forget driving eleven hundred calves down the beach in one of those years! Without the guidance of their elders, the calves ran every which way. They had little idea of moving in a herd. Some got into the waves and were drawn out to sea, sucked down the slope of the beach by the receding waves. Someone had to stay in the water to bring them back, over and over again. Other calves ran up the small streams that trickled down into each cove. Still others ran back the way we had come. It was funny and infuriating both, and it was the slowest trip I ever made moving cattle down the beach.)

The fact is that we were always overstocked when the dry years came, since no one seemed to accept the fact that there was a fairly regular pattern of two or three wet years, then a couple of medium years, followed by two or three dry years. When the dry years came, Grandfather seemed to feel that something was wrong as he struggled to decide between buying feed and selling some of the cattle. I agree with my mother that the Chumash Indians, who were there before us, would have known that the dry years were as normal as the wet ones. For some reason, even though my grandfather had been born on the ranch, he could not grasp this reality. Somehow he continued to delude himself that he could do as he felt best, even though nature was telling him something different.

Perhaps one reason why floods and wildfires are compelling for me has to do with the clarity of nature's message. On the ranch, too little rain suggested a need to reduce the number of cattle, but a wildfire demanded it. A flood rising, rising, brings us to our knees as a heavy rain does not. We can continue about our business unaffected in a heavy storm, thanks to such inventions as buildings, cars, and umbrellas. When a flood rises, however, we are returned to the attitudes of our ancestors and the realization that nature has the ultimate power. We do what we can to mitigate the physical effects, but our psychological reactions of fear and horror are no different from those of first man. If we permit ourselves these feelings, we may be able to reexperience our old respect and awe of nature and thus bring ourselves back into a feeling for the sacred power that contains us.

We do not have to carry the responsibility for everything. But one huge responsibility we do have is to make offerings to nature, whether in the form of sacrificing financial gain from timbering, or giving up our freedom to rip up the landscape with machines, or refraining from taking over dwindling virgin areas for development. In some cases, we need to sacrifice our "right" to use certain areas at all. As my mother points out, we "civilized" tend to be fascinated by a linear approach to life: we strive for advancement, progress, more of everything, and we never look back. The Chumash knew how to live on the land we ranched; they knew about growing and dying, rising and falling. They burned the land to get more grass yet were not in violation of nature; they had learned their method from nature's own fires.

We ranchers had an attachment to the land that was different from the Indians.' The Indians were in and of the land; they were respectful and careful in their relationship to it. We, on the other hand, were returnees to the land. The Europeans who came to America settled on virgin land and undertook to defeat it, to bring it under control, as had been done in their homelands. By the time my great-grandfather arrived in California in 1851, the pattern for ranching was based on the control of nature. My grandfather was immersed in the ranch from birth; he did protect the wildlife in order to preserve the balance of nature, but he also learned his father's attitude: take command of the land and make it pay enough for the family to live on. Somehow this is a contradiction in terms; the principle of linear development collides with the principle of cycles. So there was a perpetual feeling of worry: Will there be enough rain? Will a disease hit the cattle herd? Will cattle prices hold? Will the winds carry away the crops? (One year an entire mesa of small white beans was blown out to sea.) A "good" year was never experienced as that except in retrospect. We seemed always to be fighting nature.

Surely the Chumash suffered at the hands of nature, but I doubt that they fought nature. I imagine that they just pulled themselves together and rebuilt whatever had been destroyed. Destruction—including fire—was part of nature.

But for us, the reminders that nature had the last word were shocking every time. Our persistent romantic and nostalgic attitudes were as frail against the windmills of nature as was Don Quixote against his windmills. Yet tilt at them we ranch families continued to do, until finally our own civilization defeated us. How I fear the same for our wilderness!

There is a tendency among those who love the land to take elemental damage to it personally. The damage caused by a fire or flood seems like a threat, an annihilation, a personal assault—as did the dead part of the year, the end of summer after six months of no rain, to us on the ranch.

My mother wonders whether life is personal and death, impersonal. As I see it, entering into life, being born, is the beginning of an individual existence and thus is a personal time. Dying is a return to the collective state, "ashes to ashes, dust to dust," thus impersonal. Certainly I have always felt that way about the dead and dusty time before the rains begin; somehow it offends me.

11

A Ride on the Beach

~ Jane ~

The coastline of the ranch is like the floor plan of my life; perhaps that is true of any childhood place. I think that may explain the exuberance and energy I felt on a December day in 1962, as I started off on another ride.

An inch of rain had fallen, the first since a freakish late-summer storm. The earth, swollen by the raindrops after so much dryness, had taken on that curious quality of softness of light and air: softness laid on softness. Savoring the atmosphere from astride my horse, I was struck by still another dimension. It was the horse's soothing, swaying single-foot. A soft, gentle world! If only so fair a land need not be sold. But then, why should one be bound to any special place? There was Thoreau, for example, whose poetic descriptions of a small, unspectacular place had become famous for all time.

The superintendent had said, "One inch of rain goes into the earth a whole foot and can save the grass." He conveyed to me that every blade of grass had a right to live. It was as if the future of the wild growth were indistinguishable from his own. His optimism stood against his more usual silent sadness, and there was a lot to be sad about. He was that kind of man. People who lived on this place cared so much, too much.

The preponderance of browns still persisting was added to by the darkness of wet ground. The winter color scheme contrasted dramatically with the lighter autumn browns of the previous trip. Faint flecks of green, showing up overnight, had turned almost immediately into light brush strokes of sprouting grass. A pale blue sky, grayed in patches by thin mackerel clouds, brightened things high up. The clouds promoted hopes of more rain.

At the railroad crossing, I cursed the broken gate that led to the beach. Too much weight on its hinges had made it sag, and I had to drag it open. The gate, held together with rusting wire, would never be fixed. The ranch could no longer afford unnecessary maintenance. "You can get through it, and it keeps the cattle off the tracks," they told me. Although the gate had been worn down by more than sixty years of service, one could say it was still defiant, like poverty-stricken respectability. Its heavy timbers, large bolts, and general massiveness, no longer affordable, still showed.

At the beach, the rubbish had piled up tenfold. It was man-made stuff brought ashore by storm currents originating far out at sea. The amount of local precipitation did not warrant so much disturbance. Refuse from the oil platforms offshore and from the fleet of small boats servicing them was everywhere. Heavy timbers, chewed and worn by water and studded with bent, rusty spikes, must have been pried loose by the violence of the storm. Lesser logs were scattered in disarray. Plastic containers, orange and white ones mostly, were also strewn on the beach. In my childhood, stormy weather would tear kelp from the beds offshore and throw mounds of it on the beach. By summer the mounds would be washed out to sea or covered over with white sand. But no longer.

It was half tide, but because of the pushy offshore storm, it could have been high tide. Storm waves and swells, remaining below the surface long after everything had subsided, still drove the water high onto the beach. Blackbirds, foreigners to sand and seaweed, strode around purposefully, their tails angled saucily. The killdeer remained in constant alarm.

Suddenly, inexplicably released from the distressing disturbance underfoot, I felt the unbelievable freshness of the air, the slight wind in my hair, and, best of all, my lovely, big horse's single-foot pace, his body swinging like a rocking chair. Sitting on his strong back with not a soul to say yes or no, I exulted in a sense of limitlessness. But I knew it absolutely for what it was when I had to dismount to open another old gate. One's heaviness when on foot in wild places, with nothing for support, has always to be reexperienced. Mounted again, however, and soaring back into freedom, I could forget for a while the past two nights spent arguing with family members the pros and cons of liquidation.

The beach, dirty as it was, still meant freedom. The thought of the inch of rain that had fallen the day before was also freeing. The wind, from the north as it typically was after a storm, blew over the beach cliffs, leaving quiet below. The sun was hot and burning on my arms. Beyond the ocean breaker line, every kind of seabird swarmed and swooped.

Once it was clear that we were headed away from home, the horse's easy stride gradually gave way to his familiar reluctance. Old-time cattlemen would never have put up with him: a slash of the long ends of the reins across his rump, and that would have been the end of his nonsense. But my sympathies were with my wise old horse; besides, he amused me. Talking to him savagely and laying onto his rump a love tap from my quirt, I continued to admire his assertion of his individuality. He was having his own way. No wonder he had managed to live so long, looking barely middle aged.

An orange train with a glassed-in observation deck came by, announcing early afternoon time. It was northbound and apparently in no hurry. Sluggish in its ironclad way, it personified the paradox of mass, weight, immovability, and motion.

Snipe, their backs a soft gray, their bellies white, sped over the sand. In flight, they uttered tiny alarms. Sea urchins, thousands and thousands of them, were scattered over the beach. That so many of them had been thrown up by the storm saddened me. Each step my horse took made a crunching sound. Those that were spared would be drawn back into the breakers to be smashed into small pieces, ending up as a thin, gray line at high tide. The storm must have come at a vulnerable time in the sea urchins' life cycle. Many bright reddish-orange starfish, concentrated around the Bulito's eastern point on solid rock and kelp, also had been strewn arbitrarily around. Most of them were dead but not yet pale and stiffened by the sun. Their bright coloring against the slick fish-green of the kelp surprised me. The sand had gone out to sea with the storm, baring solid rock ribs and kelp and making the footing dangerous for my horse.

The hot sun did not rub out the mild, wintry feeling of damp, moving air. Summer-hot, it kept its winter character. A gentle suggestion of darkness in the bright light, like an undercoat preserving the winter depth, saved it from its midsummer superficiality. The added dimension contrasted with the transparent summer noonday that exposes everything. The soft mid-afternoon hoots of an owl from the eucalyptus grove in the Bulito was not the sleepy call of someone disturbed; it was, instead, a recognition of winter as the nighttime of the year. The mystery of the deep canyon was in the owl's relaxed voice. The scene felt like a painting that was subdued and subtle, its figures moving about in the half dusk. This was *the* season on this stretch of coast, and I was happy.

The black-and-white seabirds with the unlikely name of black turnstone were there in numbers. What an impersonal name for a nice bird—a name no better than a number! Nor does his harsh flight call justify it.

Half-tide waves were knocking against the breakwater; because of their angling, they had left a fair-sized sand space at the breakwater's point. My horse, not bothering to sniff or snort, was undisturbed by the churning water that covered the slippery rocks. He was content to stand still and meet each wave as it came to us.

At the little island of sand against the breakwater wall, I was suddenly jolted by seeing the longest sea lion I had ever seen, covered with sand and apparently dead. He was stretched out, nosed up to the foot of the wall with his tail barely out of reach of the breakers. So big and so dirty and apparently very old, he could have been twelve feet long. He had an interesting hump on his long aquiline profile. Later I realized that because of his Roman nose and lack of protuberance, "he" was a female elephant seal. Her grizzled head was unlike the smooth, sleek black heads of the sea lions in the breakers, who parallel you out of curiosity like big dogs.

Looking intently down at her from a few feet away, then leaning as far as I could from the saddle for a still-closer look, I tried to take in the extent of the motionless body. Suddenly the near eyelid flickered, opening a crack and then wider to reveal a wild black eye. Alarmed and hostile, apparently expecting no quarter from us, she threw back her head and, with opened jaws, hunched herself onto her flipper "elbows" and let out an angry bellow. She bellowed like a bull and a large, threatening dog all in one. A message from another world, from *the* other world! The animal's cry, deep throated—the essence of wilderness—also had in it a defensive, unearthly snarl. Her red throat and mouth contrasted savagely with her sand-paled body. Rows of teeth and black whiskers added to the huge power. The phrase "big as life" suddenly took on meaning. Then, mustering her strength, she rose and with unexpected agility whirled toward the breakers.

The huge animal thrashed her way out through the shallow water to the first wave big enough to carry her. As a sea lion would, she looked back, but probably not out of curiosity. All of this happened so fast that my horse had time only to make one neat, sidelong jump out of the way. Once clear, he fell back into his meandering mood, too old to be surprised for long.

Thinking over the incident, I remembered that the elephant seal had been thick and heavily muscled and well over the size of a man. A life form so much larger than man takes on more importance. Had it been a man lying there, I would have been less shocked. The seal's motionless, giant body had a strange effect on me. It was as though I had intruded on a secret, forbidden, even indecent, moment. Hurt or helpless, this animal, more able than man to cope with life's vicissitudes, should not have been caught in such a predicament. It made me wonder how big-game hunters could bear to shoot down their huge victims. Why did they not feel a terrible guilt deep down in them somewhere? That they risked their own lives was not enough justification. At first, witnessing the elephant seal had been like experiencing the demise of a famous personage, or seeing him unaware or asleep in his bed. The strangest part of all had been my involuntarily thinking of the giant animal in human terms.

Still later, I found out that these big seals cover themselves with sand for protection against the drying sun. But at the time the animal's enormous size had made me think it had lost out to some younger bulls or been shot by an angry fisherman. Besides, it had showed the cantankerousness of an old animal; and because, I thought, it was too old for mating, it must have been more interested in a safe place to hide. An old animal, unable to run away, also would likely be more dangerous: it would stand its ground and take you on, with whatever energy was left, to fight to the death. There had been time even to think of how ruthless nature can be. But perhaps life was no different for most people in Western civilization, who, when faced with death, have to meet their inner psychic enemies, including their fear of death.

After the episode, the horse, quite unperturbed, picked his way little by little through the rushing waves. I stopped him to allow each wave to recede enough to reveal the rocks. I had forgotten that a horse can afford the loss of at least one foothold.

The tide book, as interpreted by the superintendent, put low tide at 8:30 A.M., and it was just past noon at Bulito Point. The farther north one goes from Los Angeles, the later the tide. For instance, low tide in San Francisco that day came at 11:00 A.M. According to these calculations, we were rounding the point at half tide; yet the water kept welling up to the breakwater wall. I had forgotten the four-foot plus and minus tides forecast by the tide book for that particular day.

At the Santa Anita's cove, a mass of oil pipes extended to a platform in the ocean. At the Sacate, there was an underpass big enough for a horse. Strewn on the sand were many more sea urchins. These were bigger and tougher than those at the Bulito's beach. When dropped, they bounced without breaking. The biggest shells were uninhabited, but the small ones were still closed off, with life inside. My attention, however, was focused more on the waterworn rocks. They were drawing me like magnets; I must have been reaching down to my own bedrock.

Mud hens, looking more chic than their name suggests, were busying themselves at the Santa Anita's lagoon. They were a contrast to the few contemplative ducks among them. The mud hen, always darting here and there, is shining black, with a white patch on its head, stylishly placed. The ducks among them were mottled in brown, with just as surprising broad, white streaks at eye level. But they, unlike the mud hens, slipped craftily out of sight behind a bank at our approach.

Tinges of green showed up on the tawny gray hills, high up in protected swales that were warmed by the sun. Off the Santa Anita's cove, just beyond the breakers, the large, conical buoy and a raft, probably marking the oil pipes, rode the swells. On and swimming around them was the usual congregation of sea gulls.

The helicopter that was always present for the oil platforms was at last drowned out by the storm-swollen sea and noisy breakers. One blue heron, his neck stretched out to sea, stood on the high bluff. Too conspicuous, he quickly and pointedly flapped away. Tiny streams of shale flowed, without provocation, like water down the cliff face. And a large, brown bird unknown to me sounded his deep, liquid call. The stranger must have been a migrant.

We came into the huge cove fed by the Sacate, Coyote, and La Cuarta creeks, and my horse scrambled up the earthen bank below the railroad tracks. Immediately the shells and stones I had collected lost their luster. Pale and dried out on land, no longer supported by the sea, they had lost their charm. Spread out casually over the sand in naturally graceful designs and among the lesser shells and pebbles, they had conveyed their meaning. But now, with the broken shells missing, the perfect ones I had collected were no longer perfect. The best cannot be best all by itself, it seems. Once more I was forced to realize the importance of context.

The tide, too high to allow us to get around Bulito Point, sent us home overland, but the railroad's gates were padlocked. We were being ruthlessly snubbed. The railroad had impertinently shut us out. We were being deliberately belittled before our time was up!

Reduced to taking the longer way around, I saw the country as a giant pencil sketch. Its gentle shading covered the waiting color and warmth of life. Life indeed was below the surface: not only in feeling but in fact, when one considered the tons of seed lying in the soil ready to sprout. But company business had been scheduled at Gaviota, and I was expected to be there. Still in the mood of my ride, nevertheless, I was rewarded by the quiet, peaceful evening, which made me linger on the road. The Mexican cattle, grazing contentedly, exactly matched the soft evening light. Down on the mesas, as they had been earlier, they had briefly spurred my hope for more rain. Like them, even the birds seemed unhurried in the short twilight that left one suddenly to face darkness.

All in all, the elements were loving the coast. "Love" can be a pretentious word, but it adequately expressed the enfolding, bathing subtlety of the evening's gold wash, which stretched beyond imagination. The evening was made of the thinnest silk.

12

THE HORSE

~ LYNDA ~

What was it that made riding the best way to travel on the ranch? My mother describes the lift in spirits she experienced setting off on her horse to explore the ranch. I have a faded snapshot of me riding out of a corral on Cowboy, Grandfather's stud horse, looking back over my shoulder with an expression of sheer delight.

I remember starting out on cold, foggy mornings to round up cattle. The horses move crisply and eagerly, tails swishing, ears flicking forward and back. No one spoke, of course, so there was no interference to my absorption of my surroundings: the dampness of the new morning, the soft sounds of horses' hooves in the dust, the alarms set off by blue jays, the sad call of mourning doves. Warm in my jacket, I would wriggle with the excitement of the roundup, but even more affecting were the strong smell of my horse, his rolling walk, and his liveliness under me.

As my mother says, it was a liberation to be up on my horse; I was freed from my gravity weight. He and I flowed along together. It must be that sensation that prompted the image of the centaur. I felt integrated into my horse; we were all-in-one in our motion along the road.

Being on horseback brings me back to myself; I am necessarily aware of my physical state of balance, of swaying in rhythm with my horse, of the breeze in my face, of the reassuring pressure of my feet on the stirrups and my seat against the cantle of the saddle. I am held by horse and saddle even as I hold the horse steady between my knees and with my hands on the reins. The mutuality between my horse and me reassures as it enlivens.

Because of my horse I can extend myself into the physical world, literally and figuratively. I can let him take care of footing and locomotion while I consider the environment, the conditions and activity around us. He is my companion, guardian, and charge. We look after each other—if not as broadly as did the careful mare who brought her drunken rider home, at least in the sense of mutual awareness. I try to ease my weight on his kidneys by keeping my body forward on his back, except in descending steep hills, when I lean back to lighten the load on his front end. If the saddle slips forward or backward, I reseat it, and I monitor the cinch so that it does not become loose and chafe him.

We talk to each other through reins and bit, making slight pullings and tuggings to communicate about direction, speed, and obstacles. His ears are expressive, constantly conveying the direction of his atten-tion—including, sometimes, one ear forward to the path and one back toward me. The only time he lets his ears go slack is when we slide into a somnolent state while plodding along behind a herd of cattle or settle into a long walk down the beach. And even then, in his capacity as guardian, he can come to full attention at once if need be. If a bird suddenly flies up under his nose, or a cow wanders away from the herd, or a big wave washes up under his feet, he is instantly alert. His whole body gathers and flexes, and it is hard to tell whose adrenaline surge I feel, his or mine. Together we face whatever it is that startled him.

There is some parallel between the ranch child's wish to ride and his or her wish to drive a vehicle. I remember the excitement of driving the hay truck around the corral when I was about ten, while the men forked the hay off the back to the weaner calves. These forlorn little animals had just been separated from their mothers, and they would drift around the big corral as I maneuvered the truck. It was a fair obstacle course to keep the truck moving without hitting any of them. But the whole process was done in low gear, so we went very slowly, and I never did bump a calf.

California law still allowed fourteen-year-olds to get driver's licenses then, so when I became fourteen I began to drive the family car. I still enjoy driving enormously. I feel a sense of independence and mobility when driving, as I do on horseback. But many dimensions are lacking. On horseback, the sounds and smells are natural, even though not always pleasant. On the highway, one is constantly assaulted by the presence of other vehicles, fumes, and engine noise. My car does not pay attention to me, or look after me, as my horse does. The only life my car has is what I put into it. My horse, in contrast, infuses me with life.

The wilderness plays a role in my satisfaction on horseback. For a while I rode English saddle in San Francisco's big Golden Gate Park, and that was a very different experience from riding on the ranch. Because of the stable's insurance requirements, I had to have someone accompany me. Also, the park was full of people and vehicles and the paths were well defined. There were some nice vistas of gardens and lawns, but everything was supervised and controlled by park personnel. There was no sense of wilderness. The closest to wilderness we came was when riding along Ocean Beach, a pleasant stretch of wide, hard sand with an expansive view out to the shipping lanes. But still, there was a lot of traffic above the beach, and there were so many people on the beach that I felt constantly deflected from my relation to the natural setting and to my horse. Even the continuous line of container ships steaming in and out of San Francisco Bay was a contradiction to an experience of the ocean's infinity. All seemed clogged with the doings of mankind.

On the ranch, I did not mind riding out with my cousins or the cowboys. In fact, my horse went more readily if there was at least one other person along. The key was that we were all attuned to our setting and to our individual experiences of it. We did not interact with each other; we were just companions connected to our horses and our purpose. And the setting, unlike the city park, was bigger than we were. On the ranch, there was no possibility of commanding our terrain; we could only enter into it. Our command was over only ourselves, our horses, and our cattle, and it was highly imperfect at that. It would be truer to say that we were in collaboration with ourselves and our animals. As far as the land and the weather were concerned, we were, of course, only tolerated by nature.

On the ranch, if it did not rain, the range withered. In the city, if it did not rain, sprinklers were turned on in the parks. If gophers or rabbits raised havoc on the mesas of the ranch, the mesas suffered. In the city, gophers and rabbits were controlled. We were on the ranch on sufferance. The reverse is true in the city: the parks are there on sufferance.

The qualitative difference between riding in a park and riding on the ranch remains with me, even though I can no longer ride out on a roundup. The image had been imprinted in my soul and is a permanent reference point for me of harmony and perspective. Memories of those long days on horseback will always remind me that I belong to nature, rather than the reverse.

I have found that this attitude has had a beneficial effect on my health, too. Although it was not a conscious knowledge at the time, I realize in retrospect that during my childhood I understood that medical help was hours away and that we children needed to stay healthy and sound. It took three hours to drive to the nearest doctor, and on rainy days, when the ranch road was impassable, there was no way to get to a doctor at all. Without anyone spelling it out, we just knew we had better not get sick or break any bones.

Perhaps it was just coincidence that we children so rarely required medical help. I think, rather, that we knew we were on our own and as a result were more attentive to our own safety. Partly that meant developing the same sort of respectful, alert relationship with nature that an animal has. We sought harmony with the environment, yielding to the directives of weather and the demands of physical phenomena. We learned to accommodate and adapt, to roll with the punches, as it were. I remember the day I learned to let myself literally be rolled by a wave, giving up my previous mode of battling the current and the swirling turbulence. Misjudging a wave's motion as I tried to ride it in, I suddenly realized how much easier on me it was to let the wave take me under and turn me this way and that. I learned to tolerate not knowing which way was up and to trust that I would be spat up onto the beach before I ran out of air. No one taught me to do this; the understanding came by accident. But I was so impressed by how much easier it was to relax into a phenomenon than to fight it that I adopted the mode as a general attitude.

Perhaps that attitude saved me from broken bones all those times when I was thrown from a horse. Especially in the early years, I fell off horses all the time, and never did I get more than a bump or a bruise. It was not a conscious choice to let myself fall; somehow my body seemed to have learned to let it happen without a fight. Some deep trust in natural phenomena seemed to take over.

To this day, if I get a minor physical symptom, it is my instinct to tolerate the symptom even as I complain about it. It is my experience that my body, like my horse, is my companion, guard, and charge. If I listen to its signals, accept its complaints, and attempt to determine and correct what is disturbing it, my body, like my horse, will smooth out and become harmonious with me again.

What does not work for me is to attack a problem, whether the problem is with my body, my horse, or my environment. I think the long years of ranch life were instrumental in my learning to distrust attack as a way to cope with a problem.

I remember on a hot day in childhood being told to get off my horse and move a drowsy old bull from a ravine where he was holed up in the shade of some low willow trees. The men laughed at my feeble efforts to get him moving by shouting at him. "Get a stick and poke him!" they said. I did so, but the bull simply ignored the tiny stabs I administered. I became desperate; it was humiliating to fail at this simple chore. Finally, I danced all around the bull, calling to him and raising a cloud of dust. To my amazement, he hauled himself to his feet and followed me out onto the trail. I was thunderstruck and could not understand what had moved him. I still do not know; I had given up my attack on him and was just behaving haphazardly; apparently that intrigued him, or irritated him, enough that he was willing to leave the willows. As I jumped hastily back on my horse, afraid the bull might charge me, I felt thrilled to realize that the two-thousand-pound bull had *consented* to move for me. The lesson for me was that results can sometimes be drawn forth when a direct attack fails. I realize now that certain circumstances require attack, and I would not hesitate were I directly threatened. By the same token, I would plunge into an attack if someone I cared about were threatened. But in the wilderness, an attack by animals or weather would elicit evasive maneuvers from me; I would seek protection or shelter rather than counterattack.

The happiness of those "horse days" on the ranch grew out of our collaboration. My horse and I teamed up in our physical exertion and in our feelings of well-being and shared purpose. My energy seemed to enhance his experience, as his enhanced mine.

13

THE GRANDCHILDREN

~ JANE ~

I have recently been contemplating a horse ride I took with my granddaughters when they were very young, in February 1963. They had driven to the ranch with me for a short stay. I felt it important that they get a glimpse of their heritage, and, if possible, tuck in some experience of nature, which is fast disappearing.

"I am so excited!" Claudia said, again and again. She was only seven, and it was her first ride. Since she had been raised in suburbia so far, it was inevitable that city existence was for her normal; visiting wild country, therefore, must have been like visiting the zoo. But this time she was the inmate. Everything was backside-to for her.

I remembered how my twin brother and I had been, for our entire childhood, wrapped in similar excitement, so I knew that there was more to the excitement than novelty. We had been just as turned around, but we never knew it because there was no one around to explain. I felt that watching Claudia and her sister, Karen, on this trip, besides giving me the pleasure of their enjoyment, would help me get more reliable clues to my own childhood and perhaps revive some of my lost memories. I looked forward to our several days together.

Claudia had an unusual empathy for animals that her nine-year-old sister, Karen, did not. Still, the tension in both of them was the same. Excitement named the day! Thinking about this, I realized how visitors from the city must have seen my twin and me through the zoo-visitor eyes, discounting our constant state of exuberance as only childlike, even childish. Their reactions had left me vaguely aware of not being understood and not knowing why. At least Claudia and Karen had me there trying to understand.

Clint and I, sensing the burden that was on us but too little to justify ourselves, never could complain about our predicament. We were too young to articulate what adults to this day do not know, namely, that the wilderness does have a special effect on those exposed to it in childhood.

This encounter with the grandchildren would help me in still another way. Their awe and wonder would make my own notes seem less an indulgence; instead, perhaps, they would become a necessity— at least not something to apologize for. Perhaps my feeling of embarrassment and my sense of guilt for so much caring in those notes would also dissolve.

For some time I had been experiencing firsthand how one's deepest emotions arise when in one's childhood environment, especially if it is as isolated and beautiful as mine. If there is no one with whom to share these outpourings, they must go elsewhere—in my case, into my notebook. Added to my natural reactions was the threat of liquidation, which forced me into a conscious experiencing of the ranch all in a lump and late in my life. The pressure of the situation exaggerated the process of assimilation.

The behavior of these two young children was proving to me, more than ever, how crucial is the effect of wilderness and how important it is to understand the phenomenon. I could see then that my notes were not exercises in indulgence, that they might have a purpose larger than my own efforts to understand my tie to this place.

The grandchildren, being so young, were in seventh heaven, experiencing freshly the countless small happenings I had long ago forgotten. But I knew that they would not remember most of what happened. Once the incidents were taken out of context, their memories would dissolve into a blur. Inevitably, wilderness takes the human child beyond "civilized" limits, making recall difficult.

That day, nevertheless, I was helping them to be aware of what was happening by means of my own associations. As I did so, I could, at least in a general way, authenticate for them what they were living. They would not need to feel as alone as my brother and I had when we were little.

Observing them swept up in their euphoria made me realize again that had my brother and I been with understanding people like the Chumash—who were our geographical grandparents, as I was the children's real grandparent—we might have made more of what we encountered, and remembered more. Through the traditional legends, we might have remained sensitive and articulate about nature in all the subtle and small variations that were on our scale before we outsized them. The smaller and younger the child, the more eye contact counts, and the more detailed is the child's observation and appreciation. We might have allowed to emerge in us even the Indian's reverence for insects. What a wealth of awareness could have been our heritage! I also might not have had to return, month after month, in my old age to revive the endless subjective reverberations from the privacy my horse gave me.

In my youth, the wilderness had never counted with adults as it has with subsequent generations of nature lovers. Pioneers who cultivated the land and built houses on the frontier wrote in their journals, "There was nothing there"! The frontier was only an adversary to be defeated, conquered, and made ready for the application of a foreign culture.

On this day, not only were the granddaughters sensing the small happenings around us, they were also reacting indignantly to their horses' wills being set against them. (Willfulness is inevitable in horses when they find their riders uncertain.) The children were also hoping to see a puma, as I had years before. The sighting of a puma, like disaster or greatest luck, would undoubtedly be imprinted into their memories.

Unknowingly, they seemed to be reaching for something that would stick to them.

Deciding against the difficulties of the canyon, the children routed us over the mesas. Flocks of meadowlarks, restless birds, took off with distress calls at our coming. For some reason their butter-yellow breasts shone more than ever before, the black Vs marking them richly in velvet. On the ground, they glowed. Around us, the air did not move at all; everything was resting deeply after the week's rain.

Our voices seemed near and clear, as though particles obstructing sound had been washed away. The swollen earth softened the sound in the way heavy velvet drapes in a room stop confusing echoes. Everything had the quality of nearness, a living presence in the quiet. Birds, absent the month before, were everywhere. Hundreds of them, talkative ones, were around the buildings in the canyon on our return home. They seemed to have been released at last by the recent storm. There was no runoff anywhere, so surprising on a land accustomed to harsh droughts and burning winds and heat that singes. "No runoff at all," the ranch people kept saying. Everywhere, everything was gray, soft, and safe.

In an analytical mood, I noticed that the balmy air characteristic on that coast came with the onshore winds, especially the rain winds that skimmed the dampness off the ocean. Nowhere else on the California coast do the winds angle in this way. This east-west section of the coast is the only stretch where the lands are linked to the sea directly, as an adjunct, not as a division, although the aridity of the place made a strange elemental contrast. Yet that was exactly its charm: the subtropical and the semi-arid, with humidity holding them together in the constantly circulating air. It was a winter phenomenon, my favorite. In the summer, the prevailing north wind merely enforced the aridity.

Doves were distantly calling from all directions. Like the meadowlarks, they were restless and scattered. The owls could be heard in mid-afternoon; according to the locals, they were just now hatching out their young. The owls' calls were deep, dark, caressing, an otherworldly sound that one loves and eagerly listens for. Their sounds are strange, in the sense of a night call in daytime. These softened sounds from the tall eucalyptus trees fit perfectly the mothlike quality of the great horned owl as it slides noiselessly, swift as a bullet, not touching a leaf.

In the bright winter light, the owls' voices felt so good; if the young were hatching, "Mother" and "Father" might have been reassuring them. Their deep-throated, strange, eerie, shadowy, soft hooting (a watchman's periodic signal) told me that all was well for them in this hostile sunlit world. But why should these night birds, quiet in daytime for the rest of the year, be active now? Did their parental-courtship rituals carry them over into the day? I had heard two of them in the canyon late in the day before, echoing each other. Were they latecomers in the domestic season?

I felt sad that I had to record these observations to myself; the children would not, perhaps could not, join me on this level. Action was "it" for them. Yet somewhere in their systems a taste for so much beauty might lodge. A taste for nature at least might take hold. It was worth the overall effort on my part, I thought.

The three of us rode along, talking and joking, the children from their centers and I from mine, but somehow connecting. I did see, in spite of the pleasant distraction, that the San Augustine was green, the giveaway sign of the beginning of spring growth, not the end of it. The chartreuse effect that had persisted so long after the maximum growth last year was missing. Gentle, tentative moods surviving the midwinter drought contrasted sharply with the previous year's violently productive spring growth. In spite of the children's high spirits, I drank in the tender, light-bathed quality of the place. Yet I knew, from past experience, that spring in the normal sense, would never catch up, no matter how much more rain fell. The vegetation depends too much on the actual calendar reading.

Tired, we came back from El Cojo the easy way, by the beach. We came onto an elephant seal, dead and rotting—the same one I had seen alive on the previous trip. The seal had been ill or wounded after all, and near death, when she had made that last violent effort to survive.

Cornered by her own weakness, the animal had put every ounce of herself into that enraged bellow. I tried to describe the awful sound to the children, but for them the seal was a dead thing to be avoided. No doubt because of its size as much as its deterioration, it was outside their capacity to experience. They wanted no part of it.

A black, ducklike bird known as a surf scooter, flopping its way out to sea, acted as though it were injured and, like all frightened ducks, ruffled its top knot. Coal-black, with a bright white patch on the back of its head and with more white on its face, it had a heavy, red bill.

Our Norwegian elkhound was with us; it was her first experience of ranch life. She had never seen horses before, and as she ran along the beach following us, she riveted her attention on us high up on our horses and let out little barks, her large, luminous eyes questioning. It was what she always did when running alongside the car, wanting to get in.

As I thought more about what the girls experienced that day, I had to conjecture that a similar mind-blotting excitement must have smothered me as a child, too. Although we were experts in our environment, my brother and I were inarticulate in the civilized sense. (For instance, all my life I have kept a dictionary next to me when I read; I do so to this day.) Perhaps someday, I thought, our society might turn the experience of raw nature—which, in my generation, was thought of as a primitive and therefore regressive influence—into a broadening of some sort by promoting the expressions of children's reactions and feelings in nature, regardless of what they are. My granddaughters' aroused and heightened feeling of excitement, so similar to my own childhood excitement, surely came out of normal, deep, inner psychic levels—a reservoir of energy and emotional potential that could be touched by what surrounded us. I speculated whether the effect of wilderness in childhood might not need to be limited if it was not to end in a near-total rubout. Someday, perhaps, what children could tell us would be translated into a valid part of nature's meaning. I hoped so. The child's awe of, and fascination with, wildlife, preserved throughout life, might help to save our wilderness from destruction.

I felt that we three—Claudia, Karen, and I—had been plunged into what I have already described as a spaceless, timeless, priceless eternity, something that need not be ours alone.

That day of rapport with the small girls also helped me to think about where I was heading. Having small girls as reminders, whatever the context, could help me in my old age, with its lessened ego, to visualize the broader vistas of hope that are not normally the province of the ego. I would try to get an inkling of the creative forces such as those that underlay the children's exuberance. Old people and children, after all, similarly lack ego. The child is not ready for one, and the old person no longer has much need of it. The old and the very young together, as we were that day, might tell all of us something we need to know.

There had been something beyond comprehension in the offing that day for all three of us. Now I could make sense of my granddaughters' hilarity: the children had only been transliterating into laughter what they did not, or could not, articulate. It had been clear to them, however, that "something" had grabbed hold of them, and they had seemed reassured by my repeated "Yes, yes, I know."

I think that the "something" all of us resonated to was, for lack of a better explanation, the coast as a thing-in-itself, a living spirit just then creating niches for all three of us, as it had long ago formed a lifelong trap for my twin brother and me. On that day in 1963, we three joined in with the few living on that place who were at least a little aware of its overall power—the children through their excitement, and me by means of my empathy. Someday, I hope, that power will be identified. Other people too are grabbed by it, and they also stay on the land. Perhaps all of us are caught somewhere by what is stronger than any human consciousness.

Thanks to Karen and Claudia, I can finally take seriously my brother's and my childhood excitement, exuberance, and hilarity, which, until their visit, I had never tried to understand. Now in my mid-eighties, I recall, for instance, when my twin and I first came to the ranch at the age of five and met the unusually strong winds that are characteristic of the place. They were new experiences to us. Almost immediately on arrival we deliberately challenged the winds—our aim being to lean on them. Because we were so small, we did. Each time we tried and succeeded, we laughed and laughed wildly. I remember so well playing with the winds day after day; they became a source of our happiest times. So much wind must have kept us repeating the challenges time and time again. It is therefore not surprising that now, in my old age, I can remember vividly how excruciatingly exciting the episodes were.

At this point I need to explain why, in my late fifties and early sixties, I was referring to myself as old and no longer needing the kind of ego that belongs to youth. I did indeed think a lot about death around the age of sixty. Like many other people I have known, I wondered about my end because there seemed barely enough time left to do something important, at least in my eyes. The "I" in one's thoughts, the ego, around that time of life concerns itself with the problem of mustering enough point of view and energy to achieve finally what one was meant to do, having been born into a certain context. I believe, too, that the part of one that uses the word "I," if not overcompensated and exaggerated by feelings of inadequacy, tends to fade with age.

From my present age of eighty-plus years, sixty now seems almost young. But the question of death no longer holds the forefront of my attention as it did then. I seem to have dealt with death enough to let it be part of my fate.

If one is lucky enough to get a second wind in the late fifties, a certain "Not-I" can begin to speak its piece. The "Not-I" comes out of the combination of one's genes and one's earliest context. Thoughts and meanings, observations—designs also, or melodies, depending on the person's talent—will begin to surface in an informal, unstructured way. They will not, at first, be in any form acceptable to academia or society. These small upsurges or eruptions or revelations will want to be honored and will perhaps insist on being worked over. They will have lives of their own; they can even become all-absorbing for the rest of one's life. In short, they will want out, as I mentioned above. The youthful ego must at least step aside, if it has not been dimmed in one's natural aging.

As for me specifically, I understand through my notes that my old-age thoughts may also have come out of a possible identification with the impending loss of the ranches. I felt so much a part of them, especially the coast ranch, that I felt that when they no longer belonged to us, I would also be gone, in a sense. At the least, I would psychologically die with their loss, and, I hoped, reemerge by means of knowing what they meant to me. Death certainly was in the air for me in my late fifties and sixties.

Communication and memory may very well be linked. For example, since the girls did not want to talk about the dead elephant seal (possibly because they had not seen it alive, as I had), I doubted that they would remember it. The children, although comfortable with the unusual and exceptional as part of their repertoire, would probably not remember what was beyond them. Nor would they retain whatever came to them that could not be communicated to the adults—just as the huge, dead, rotting elephant seal was also being rubbed out.

In the long run, what my brother and I had daily taken into our psychic systems, what we had lived by as much as the air we breathed, what had made us different from our city peers, was lost. Our differences from city children remained, but there was little recollection of what had led up to those differences. This loss need not have happened, it seems to me, had the adults around us known more about the psychic power of the wilderness. They could have helped us eventually to remember what we needed of our childhood so that we could value in adult terms what we had absorbed. To my mind, there is psychically within us not only the animal, but also the vegetative, layer of the experience of the wilderness. These manifest at least in dreams, and they need to be assimilated. There is also the whole self-regulating, all-inclusive psychic world exactly mirroring, and being mirrored by, the wilderness. This inner and outer resonance has not been addressed, to my knowledge, by the biologists. Poets like Henry David Thoreau and Robinson Jeffers have shown how creativity can bloom in the wild. But even they do not tell us why we are caught for life by the wilderness when we experience it for the major part of our childhood.

Instinct, perhaps from the beginning, grew out of environmental demands. In technical terms, the formation of instinct, in connection with exposure to the wilderness, has to happen at an early age. The environment imprints onto what has surfaced in the child as his genetic heritage. The earlier the child is imprinted by wilderness (wild animals, vegetation, climate, and especially the silence), the more likely his inherited primitive psychological layer, corresponding to the American Indian's cultural development, will be uppermost and able to meet the wilderness impact. In that case, the connection of instinct and environment is set for life and ensures a good relation to nature. If one believes, as Jung claimed, that the recapitulation of the history of the human race occurs psychologically as well as physically in the individual, instinct and environment become one. "Ontogeny recapitulates phylogeny." The point just might be expressed by Gregory Bateson's aphorism, "Without context, there is no meaning."

~ *LYNDA* ~

I am interested to learn of my mother's experience in showing my daughters the ranch. At that time, the children were growing up in the suburban area where my husband and I had settled some years before. The area was roomy and only partly developed, and many of our neighbors had donkeys in their backyards. But to me it was citylike and tame. Karen and Claudia ran a bit wild; I did not supervise them, just as I had not been supervised as a child. Nonetheless, their lives there were defined by neighborhood attitudes regarding property lines, household routines, and family gatherings. So they were in uncharted territory, literally and figuratively, when they arrived on the ranch with my mother, their grandmother.

Claudia, at seven, was the same age I had been when I came to stay on the ranch, but because of my mother's efforts she was not so isolated with her experience as I had been, and as my mother had been before me. Perhaps I needed to become part of my cousins' group for the same reason my mother needed to ally with her twin: a mediator is necessary to help one endure safely the power of nature. My mother's impulse to mediate for my daughters came out of her awareness of the importance of such mediation for a child in the wilderness.

I, too, remember the excitement of being on the ranch. When I was ten and my brother was seven, he and I left the ranch to rejoin our parents up north, near San Francisco. After that, our trips to the ranch were mostly limited to the three months of summer. Until I was old enough, at age fifteen, to drive us to the ranch, we came down by train. Since the nearest train station was south of the ranch, in Santa Barbara, we had first to travel the whole distance across the ranch, all along the right-of-way our great-grandfather had given to the railroad. We would press against the train windows, watching for the first sign of the ranch, then buzz and giggle and point out landmarks for the length of the crossing. The long drive from Santa Barbara and over the ranch road to my grandparents' house subdued us both; usually the carsickness and fatigue doused the excitement. By the next morning, though, we were thrilled again by our contact with the place, which had long since become our psychic home and source of renewal.

But almost at once that excitement would again be overridden, this time by our anxiety over finding our places there. My daughters were able to pin themselves to my mother, so they did not have to find their footing for themselves. Perhaps they made less of a bond with the place as a result. I agree with my mother's thought that living in the wilderness from early childhood does involve one more utterly than coming to it later in life.

Leaving the ranch at the end of summer was like pulling the plug out of the bathtub. My energies would drain away as we left the ranch road and entered the highway. I suppose I went into a sort of mourning. The idea of enduring nine months of city life before being able to return to the ranch was depressing. To this day, leaving nature to go to the city saddens me and leaves me feeling simultaneously flat and anxious.

I wonder just what the excitement of being on the ranch was all about. I felt an infusion of energy that sustained me in strenuous physical activity all day long. Rising early in the morning, sometimes before dawn, I would be awake and ready for the day. Breakfast at my grandparents' was at 5:30 A.M., and they would both be working on it by the time I came downstairs. Grandmother believed in "health food," as she called it, based on Adele Davis's books on diet. "Health food" meant a ranch grapefruit, small and sour, fried liver, and heavy multi-grain pancakes covered with blackstrap molasses. Grandfather was in charge of mixing up the pancakes; my brother and I called them "cartwheels." We did our best to eat everything, but of course it was too much, and there would be arguments about finishing. Ultimately, we would escape and leave the house. If I were going out with the men to work cattle, I would carry a lunch and not return until sunset. The days were long and hard, but tired as I would be at dinnertime, I always had enough energy. I think Grandmother's diet was only part of the reason!

On the days when I was alone, I would disappear into the environment. Often I became Tarzan; Grandmother had a complete set of Tarzan books, and I loved them. Tarzan merged with the vegetation, the terrain, and the animals and was sustained and embraced by nature. He seemed to have limitless energy and was constantly on the move. I became like that quite consciously, which may be why I remember the process so clearly, in contrast to the memory of unconscious exploration that my mother says she has lost. I cut bamboo from the grove Grandmother had planted near the Big House and made a clumsy bow and arrows. I climbed trees and swung from their branches. I tried to move without making noise, not very successfully, and was constantly on the alert for marauders.

I wonder whether excitement such as my daughters exhibited when riding with my mother is most people's experience when heading into wilderness. Or maybe we all experience an energy surge but in variable forms, depending on how old we are, how secure we feel, and how our previous experiences of the wilderness have affected us.

When I was six, I saw the Disney movie *Snow White and the Seven*

Dwarfs and was deeply terrified by the wild, black, alive night forest that clawed and scratched Snow White as she fled her malevolent stepmother's death edict. It was as if the forest were the terrifying queen incarnate. Just watching the scene, I experienced an overwhelming surge of fear. And in my early days on the ranch, I felt a similar fear coursing through me again and again. Certainly those were surges of energy, albeit negative energy.

Had young Karen and Claudia been alone on the back mesas of the ranch, they would have been just as energized as they were when with my mother, but the energy would have been felt as fear, not delight. What transformed the energy from negative to positive for them was her presence. Not only could she guide them and help them with their rambunctious horses, she could also mediate the enlivenment experience for them so that they had little to fear. But the sheer force of the enlivenment was undiminished; it was as if they had been plugged into a light bulb socket!

I can imagine that coming to raw nature as a child might activate energy levels that otherwise would remain unawakened. A child remains embedded in his family, especially his mother, unless or until something happens to bring him out of that merger. Being introduced to the wilderness can effect that disruption, if the child has an opportunity to explore. But the enormity of nature can also flood him with excitement and terror to the point of absorbing him as fully as his family had before. So he may leave the human merger and enter into a merger with nature, having little more awareness of his individual being than he did before.

This transfer of mergers may be what happened to both my mother and me. We were both turned loose in the wilderness when we were very young, with very little contact with family. Nature became the source of all energy for us, and because nature is limitless, so were the amounts of energy we felt surging through us.

And perhaps it was losing that resource when we came to civilization later that left us enervated and depressed. Like the Greek Antaeus, we had regularly to touch earth, as it were, to come alive.

So I wonder whether it makes a critical difference at what age one first experiences nature, how thoroughgoing the experience is, and how big a part the family continues to play in the child's life. Based on what happened to my mother and me and on her observations of a modified form of it in her granddaughters, I think that the level of ego development at the time nature is entered, plus the strength of the ongoing connection to adults, will determine the level of psychic energy stimulated by nature for the rest of that individual's life.

14

DROUGHT

~ JANE ~

Unfortunately, in the cattle business, long dormant periods mean bankruptcy for many cattlemen, and there is no comeback. Man's loss is different from nature's loss. Humans can be eliminated by financial losses for good, but not nature. Her life force returns as though there had never been a drought. The hard seed lying in the ground, sometimes waiting for long periods until the right conditions occur, sprouts and sets in motion the food chain. I have to admire the tenacity and hardiness of the vegetation and to enjoy the faint signs of color in the toughest flowers that hurry to ripen.

Drought conditions and desert air are affined, except that desert life long ago made permanent peace with lack of rain. Southern California cannot, because of intervening floods. Privation, especially where man is in charge, can make areas look ragged and tattered.

Around us on the ranch, the northern rain climate and the southern desert climate met. The rains were sometimes from the north and sometimes from the south. This meeting place of climates is duplicated nowhere else, so far as I know. The combination could favor us, or it could double our hazards. The ranch could become a no-man's-land between too much and too little. Added was the southern exposure, similar to that of the French Riviera. Perhaps we should have accepted as our base the desert extreme and been taken unawares, even happily inconvenienced, by unusual rainfall. Overall, we might have been less surprised and more prepared.

We often played with the thought that we could turn the ranch into a dude ranch. Few city-bred people can resist what seems to them the romantic cowboy life. Little do they know! Yet the tourist trade, eventually when all else fails the sine qua non of civilization, also marks a ranch's death, and why not? Eras have to come to an end. In California, after the Indians came the trappers and hunters of the West who, like the Indians, lived and died in nature. Then came the Spaniards, with their cattle and an approximation of Spanish culture. After them came the Yankees, with less sentiment and less feeling for nature, and with them the better but ecologically more destructive cattle.

Now, cattle were less and less a major industry. Because of the demand for coastal land, property values had risen, increasing taxes and making cattle ranching unprofitable. Ironically, overvaluation of the land, originally worshiped by the Indians, became its killer. Civilization, industrialization, and overpopulation, along with their aftermath, disregard for ecology and devastation of nature, finally became the order of the day.

In January 1964, the coast, subtly, handsomely subdued, was a portrait in brown. The browns were clear, clean, live browns, chocolate browns, soft browns. Warm tans were also there. The ever-present dark green oaks became markers in this sea of brown. In the fall a lot of rain had fallen, but by January everything had been sent back to its beginnings. The place had come out of an end-of-the-year dormancy, but within its somber colors.

The sunset from the beach reflected the long, dry winter interlude. A metallic yellow at first, it changed into the gold of gold coins—preserving the metaphor. The sun, shrouded in red verging on pink in the western mist, tinted the edges of the clouds that lay layer upon layer in the southeast. All in all, the evening shone like newly polished brass. Hard edges were everywhere in the light that streamed deep and clear into the ocean horizon, reaching all the way to the setting sun. Long, yellow shafts of light, too vivid and brilliant to look into, crossed rows upon rows of breakers hurrying to the shore. The shafts reached across the sand of a deep minus tide up to where I was standing. They blackened into silhouettes the few large, embedded rocks and some curlews and sandpipers feeding there. The metallic atmosphere of midwinter dry weather unavoidably suggested more drought. Only the brave green tints here and there on the brown hills proved there had been a wet fall.

The next day a soft breeze, faintly insinuating winter, led into the glaring mid-morning light, but there was no rain in it. A thin band of mist moved across the sky from the west against the glaring white light. It was telling us that drought must not take over totally. And that we had to make a profit in cattle in order to survive!

I had to admit, nevertheless, that the coast's uniqueness related directly to the lack of rainfall. Its overwhelming attraction came as much from the harsh conditions as from the benevolent rains, if not more so. Droughts had always been with us: three years out of ten, and at least one exaggeratedly dry. This area, besides, was officially designated as semiarid.

The twisted, gnarled oaks and snarled shrubbery, the tough sage with its delicate, tentative lavender and sometimes white flowers, in a perverse way proved the beneficence of dry years. Life, desperately but surely hanging on until the next rain, no matter how slight, gave the place an overall sense of beauty in strength. The desert cactus, a miracle of even greater tenaciousness, in the same way makes the Southwest what it is. Cactus stores water in its bulbous, fat, grotesque leaves to suit the harsh beauty of the desert. Exaggerations of design make the desert a showplace. From the beginning of time, our coast had also adapted to the problem of too little rain, but unlike the desert, except for the desert's occasional flash floods, it had to adapt to too much.

Thousands of butterflies were flying distractedly in all directions in the early light and quiet. They had survived the heavy rainfall, and in the six weeks' midwinter drought they were being given another chance. A quail called from clear across the Bulito. So far away, yet so clear, its voice was the only sound to penetrate the silence.

Mornings and evenings were the best times on the coast; high noon was flat. By late afternoon there was the slightest promise of rain, and the coast was showing off its pastels: green tints and soft, lively browns, soft sky blues, and the gray, wet sands of low tide, animated by flocks of round, whitebosomed sandpipers. The birds, uncharacteristically, were in no hurry at all. Dark green oaks on the distant hills softly accentuated the grays of the sage. Toward evening, visibility was perfect. The cliffs, frankly yellow, surprised me. Rain was officially predicted, bringing some optimism.

Streams of light from the lowering sun sparkled on the rocks and pebbles in the sand, their shadows individualizing them. They became tiny, self-important monuments. One small shorebird, his black legs blurred by his speed, steered his body around like a tiny craft. His black bill angled in anticipation toward the sand, he hardly bothered to fly at my arrival. The round-the-clock foghorn sounding from the oil platforms made no sense, but at least it was not as loud as usual. An endless freight train with six engines sent slight shock waves through the air and totaled everything with its racket.

The ocean, flat and dark blue-green, with its ever-present white breakers, faithfully followed the scalloped shoreline. Around me were rounded pebbles—symbols for all eternity, and from all eternity, saying that the moment was like one grain of sand on twenty-five miles of beach. Why be compelled again and again to describe these details? Did the infinite variety of nature warrant this, or did the threat of liquidation and modern man's progress legitimize the obsession? I did not know the answer.

Starfish were everywhere, clinging silently with their deathly grip to the rock crevices. The outgoing tide had exposed them, forcing them to hold tight. Looking naked and indecent out of water, they showed their weird colors: browns, oranges, and reds, embellished by fine white beading. One giant creature, dressed in maroon and outlined with larger white beads, was so much a part of the rock that it looked like an excrescence, yet handsome in its way. Some were in each other's arms; others seemed squashed into beds of mussels. Thousands upon thousands of big and small starfish, rows upon rows of them, literally left no space uncovered. Sea anemones barely showed up among them; a few starfish were thickly dusted over by the sand.

The shorebirds were numerous. Smaller sandpipers, their heads tucked in, were perfect replicas of the larger varieties, and just as bosomy. They speeded this way and that, their legs hardly belonging to their bodies. The legs could have been running around on their own, with bodies in tow. Bodies in small flotillas were sailing on a layer of air!

The kelp revealed by the minus tide glistened. The sun streaming across the flat sea from low on the horizon pierced it, giving it a strange amber quality. Tire tracks in the sand jarred and angered me—futilely. The old childhood feeling that I had been there first and should have priority over people like these, trespassing in their Jeeps, came back. I was reminded of when, almost a lifetime ago, a dead man had washed up on the beach. I had felt that he had no right to be there, that he was an intruder! But, of course, fishermen had trolled this coast well before I appeared, and there had been the generation before me; and before them, the Spaniards, and still earlier, the Chumash. I was out of line, but I could not shake my sense of priority. Either there was in me a hangover of the child's need to be first or I was still reacting to my unconscious childhood feeling that identified my beginning with the place.

Nature was oblivious in this matter of priority, but somehow she had a way of making us hate outsiders, always finding them in error or, in a subtle way, inferior. One could feel superior in isolation, where one's fellows' criticisms could not intervene. But I also remembered wondering sometimes why others had not noticed how superior we were!

These thoughts led to a vivid memory from early childhood of waiting outside a movie theater for someone to pick me up. Watching the stream of people coming out, I thought they were deformed! I had not seen high heels before, nor hairdos; nor did I know anything about style. Identification with nature can be as formidable as any other identification, it seems.

My twin brother and I looked upon the city child as a poor thing because he, or sometimes she, could not swing through the trees like a monkey or play tag on a six-inch board topping a network of chicken yards six feet in the air. Nor could he track an animal over broken terrain, or see anything smaller than a barn; a slight movement in the sage or a stir in the oak leaves meant nothing to him. The city child could not detect a "homing" bee and find its hive, or know about the yellow jacket bulleting its way to feast on an anomalous oak branch growth resembling an immature acorn.

The city child's ignorance and ineptness only pleased us. Ours was a secret society that excluded him. The bird and animal lore also was solely ours and contained infinite knowledge. Rooted in our earliest observations, when the smallest detail had carried momentous meaning, our reports differed radically from book knowledge. Or did our knowledge apply only to local variations? Probably not. The persistent, minute rasping sound of a tiny bird, for instance, signaled the threat of a predator. A "frozen" cottontail, seemingly glued to his thin trail, told us of the presence of a rattlesnake. Looking closer, we were sure to find the snake, imperceptibly, purposively advancing on the rabbit, his rapier tongue flipping in and out, "licking his chops" as he followed the immobilized rabbit's scent.

Our special knowledge and experience, however, took their toll later. We became imprisoned in a world devoid of contemporaries. We could not leave our context because in doing so we lost our sense of meaning, and we spoke a language that was misunderstood. Our "island" became too small to support us as adults. Our inarticulateness made us targets. We were closer to the animals than we were to human beings; as with primitive people, the animals were our "little brothers." Necessities of life by some people's standards cut down our appreciation of the aesthetic world. Nor did society's pleasures touch us. In short, in certain areas we were unconscious, undeveloped, immature, and far from superior.

On the beach, a breeze, coming steadily and gently out of the west, gave me hope. Facing into the wind and extending my right arm in line with my shoulders as my father had taught me, my right index finger pointed due north, where the storm would be. In San Francisco that evening, sure enough, it rained.

The sun, cold, brilliant, and dangerous as it set close to the ocean's edge, finally turned the evening into an aged steel engraving. The optimistic soft browns under a buff-colored sky, shaded by green tints on the northern slopes, indicated the end of spring. But the jagged peaks dominating Gaviota Ranch, with the rapidly golding cliffs in the foreground, suggested otherwise. Everything was too alive in that evening that came on so fast, with its sculpturing foreground effects, to think of trouble. The earth absorbed the cold, fading gold of the evening sun, neatly silhouetting a lone curlew.

The sagebrush was washed clean. And across the tracks, one lackadaisical frog was sounding off. He had heard the prediction of rain but was still unbelieving. There could have been moisture under the earth's surface, and the catch-dams were full, yet the green grass was short because of the cold and wind. Suddenly the sun was gone: without celebration, without sunset. The inland light was blackening perceptibly. Everything was clear and tidy and near. The silence shut down the day totally. There was nothing more to anticipate; everything was there and then. Time and life stand still in the moment of a darkening winter dusk, as they do in the curious quiet that comes at the time of dawn. There were only the distant sounds of evenly timed breakers; not a single bird sounded its way to bed. Only a distant, sleepy owl announced the long night to come. An awful burst of something should have followed so much quiet; instead, there was only one more beginning of another long, lonely winter night.

By the next day, the magic had gone. Not yet mid-morning, a brassy desert light screamed out the hot winter sun's first appearance. On the way to town for the monthly board meeting, I saw on the main ranch road a small coyote, looking more like a small, slight, alert, fuzzy dog than the wild thing I had seen so many times before. Out of curiosity he stood there, then he quietly cleared the bank and slipped away into the mustard, avoiding the car as any small dog would. Nothing magical about him that morning. Or had I had enough of the place, and was I up to date with my thoughts?

15

SOLITUDE AND SILENCE

~ *LYNDA* ~

As I remember my early ranch years, I realize how significant my experience of solitude was. It was so much more a part of my life than it would have been if I had grown up in the city. In recent years, as solitude has become harder to find, I have contemplated its place in my life, rising from that childhood experience. Inevitably, I think also about silence and its importance to what I know of solitude. And linked to those reflections is my feeling about relatedness to people and animals. These three phenomena—solitude, silence, and relatedness—are interconnected for me.

As a very small child, even before I moved to the ranch, I had considerable opportunity to be alone. Whether or not I connected with the people of the foreign countries where I lived as a child, I was always a bit "other" from them. The loss for me was feeling that I did not belong; the gain was solitude and a developing attraction for animals. I remember living for a year or so in Sussex, England, with my brother and the two middle-aged sisters who took care of us while our parents were studying in Zurich. I did not have a lot in common with my brother, who was much younger, so I often went off alone into the countryside. A dog named Judy, a smallish, furry beast who lived in the house, went with me. I remember making my way under great chestnut trees; pushing aside tall, rough bracken, a kind of dry fern; and feeling, as much as seeing, the huge expanses of bright bluebells. I felt welcome in this scene, and I was sufficiently sustained by the presence of Judy that I never felt afraid or too far from home, even though I was only six or seven at the time. Having Judy with me was like being at home.

In that country area and, later, on the ranch, silence was taken for granted. But there was a difference between the silence of the English countryside and the silence of the vast ranch wilderness. In Sussex, there were cars and people everywhere, and fences and herds of domestic animals, which maintained a sense of civilized life. But it seems to me that people had less to say in those days in rural England than we do nowadays, wherever we are. Similarly, no one on the ranch talked much, except to exchange concrete information necessary to get something done.

The only exception to this phenomenon was my grandmother. She had a great deal to say to any adult who stopped at the house. I never understood those conversations, since they usually referred to whatever book she was reading. I remember so clearly Grandmother sitting in her place on the couch in the living room; always there was a stack of three or four library books beside her. She marked her page with a rubber band stretched around the book's cover. Grandmother's life centered on her reading; she had no physical relation to the ranch at all. She never went beyond her garden except for her weekly (weather permitting) trips to Santa Barbara. There she would shop, eat in a restaurant, and go to the library.

For Grandmother, conversation was as necessary as breathing. For those brought up on the ranch, however, conversation did not exist. Grandfather, who had been born on the ranch, did not converse. Although he had been a considerable bon vivant as a young man at college and in Alaska's gold rush, he reverted to silence when he returned to take over after his parents' deaths.

I remember evenings on the ranch, when my grandparents would sit in the living room, Grandfather in his massive rocking chair by the window and Grandmother in her usual corner of the couch. She would direct a monologue to him, but he would not even look up from his newspaper or agricultural journal. In later years he became deaf, apparently. Grandmother simply raised her voice and continued her talking. It must have been necessary for her to hear her own voice, even if she received no response. I felt sad for her when I overheard her talking to Grandfather. Silence can feel like an attack, I have since come to realize. I must have sensed that then, even though I could not have articulated it. Surely it must have felt that way to her.

When I was new on the ranch, I felt silence as a criticism. As a newcomer, my position was tenuous. It did not occur to me then that I was being conditioned by people's silence, was being taught that silent was the way to be. I felt that my every remark was unwelcome and wrong, and I soon learned to be silent too. Later, as an adult in the city, I found that if I lapsed into silence in the company of others, I offended them with what they described as a passive withholding of myself.

On the ranch, relatedness developed in the silence between people. In the city, relatedness developed in the talking between people. To this day, I struggle with this disparity.

I remember the silence of the cattle roundups. As we started down the road toward whichever canyon we were working that day, each of us would be busy with his or her thoughts. At the mouth of each canyon, a couple of us would leave the group and head up the creek to bring down the cows that were all over the canyon walls. I cannot remember how we knew which canyon would be ours; we just knew.

I would start up my canyon with another person or two, and things would become even quieter: just the soft plop of horses' hooves in the dust, the occasional bird call, and the first cattle starting at our approach. The old oaks provided shade as we went along.

Silently we would continue all the way up to the back ridge that ran across all the canyons, and then we would fan out to sweep the cattle before us down to the mouth of the canyon. It would take a couple of hours to get all of them gathered into a herd at a creek at the bottom of the canyon. There I would rejoin my partner, and we would push the cattle down to the mesas, where the road was. And all this time, nothing was said. All I would hear was the clucking to the horses and the shouting at the cattle to keep them moving.

Gradually I learned to keep quiet, and to relax when I was alone. I was glad when rainy days came, or when the other children had to go to town. Those were rare occasions—it rained so little—and wonderful. I could disappear into the ranch so that even I did not know where I was. Or I could go up to the barn and be with Cowboy, the quarter horse stallion who was sire to all our cow horses.

Cowboy had a big stall and outdoor area next to the saddling shed. As I became bolder, I would go into his stall and just be with him. Sometimes I would lean on him; other times I would get up on his round back. His warm body and amiable nature gave me a soft, timeless peace.

Solitude on the beach was different from solitude inland. On the beach, where I did not have to watch for rattlesnakes and gopher holes, the smooth sand was hypnotic as I walked along.

My favorite solitary activity was to ride a horse on the beach, with just the waves and birds to keep us company. The horse would seem to share my state of merger with the place; the sense was of complete harmony. If I spoke to him, his ears would flip back at once. I had the feeling of being connected to another living being, with no conscious effort required.

Those long, silent days on the ranch formed my understanding of how to be in life. It became so natural to be silent that I literally forgot how to converse. Fifteen or so years later, my husband succeeded in teaching me to engage in conversation again. Like my grandmother, he is a highly educated, sophisticated person, well traveled and articulate; and, like her, he wanted someone to talk with. Unlike my grandparents, we settled in San Francisco, a city of education and culture. So I relearned what I had originally known: in the city, speech is relatedness.

What I forgot in relearning to talk was that silence and solitude are both part of my appreciation of the world—and that the wilderness, the place for the experience of solitude, is an essential part of my life. Now that I have finally become aware of the importance to me of solitude, I arrange for it. What seems more difficult is to regain the capacity to find solitude in the company of others, to relate in silence without seeming aloof.

I do not need to be alone much now. If I can have some interval of literal solitude every day, however, I enjoy my contact with others much more. The wilderness taught me this about myself.

16

WORDS

~ *JANE* ~

I often struggle to find words that express exactly the sense or meaning of what I am seeing. Words are like transparent containers that organize what one sees and imagines, at the same time revealing it. Words also can transform one's sensibilities into meaning. The invocation of the exact word and the organization of divergent details thus somehow have much in common. But this is how consciousness comes about! One might say that content is meaning and that the container that organizes it is the word.

My effort to fix meaningful words so they will not slither away invokes small struggles and, periodically, small, satisfying victories. Feelings also are content that can be arranged to convey significance. Writing, for me, is the digging out of meanings, feelings, and sensibilities—all the things that have to do with oneself, once neatly set aside—and putting them into a completed row of my own words.

I need to unburden or I puff up with undigested impressions. When I do not make the effort to express what is within me, what has been constellated by endless stimuli and impressions gathered over time, I become as though empty because I am overfull! My creative urge is the tool for unburdening. The unburdening in turn causes a kind of emptiness that is restful: the feeling of a job well done, something small and new under the sun delivered out of my depths.

Late in the summer of that drought year—in September 1964—I returned to the ranch and again recorded my experiences there.

I mounted poor old bored Hollywood, a horse who had been bought to substitute for our ranch-bred horses, which had been sold. It was about ten in the morning, and all the men had gone their various ways for their day off. It was important not to delay: there would be a three-foot-plus rise, even at low tide, making the space around the breakwater narrow.

Once more, I was let out of prison. The ranch wind was at its worst, or perhaps its best. Like a storm at sea, it carried moisture that promised winter. With the wind howling wildly, as a wind can only over an open ocean, Hollywood and I headed down the long Bulito Canyon. By the beach, quail ran and hid in the sage, making low, hurried, liquid clucking sounds. Their sounds reminded me of the audible whispers of small children who think they are out of sight of the adults.

Somehow the wind and the competent strength of my horse released me from the bitterness and details of my everyday life. I had felt self-conscious asking the men to saddle my horse on their day off. I had told them that I wanted to "see a certain part of the ranch," implying that the ride had to do with my duties as a stockholder and board member. I had not wanted to confess that I needed to revive my feelings and thoughts and feel the exhilaration of experiencing things that matter. How would the men have reacted if I had said, "The eternal comes on winds that yell like banshees, and the quail remind me of little children, and my horse, with his grand muscle system and knowing looks, gives me confidence"? The men would have given me the benefit of the doubt, most likely, but they would have tried to forget what I had said as quickly as possible.

Psychologists tell us that when we are close to animals, we are close to the deeper powers in ourselves: close to the instincts, where time is timeless and space is only a detail to bother with. Somehow I fell into that experience that day. I felt a connecting link with all of life, seen and unseen, a going forward with such ease and pleasure as though into eternity. On my horse the impossible was possible, and I could transcend myself. Hollywood was no black horse of destiny—he was a pinto, a bay marked crazily in white. But that did not matter. Hollywood was in rapport with me and I with him. We were on a joint venture.

At the railroad crossing at the Bulito, the ancient, bedraggled pine tree, planted many years ago, that once had stood as an important symbol in my dreams of the ranch seemed more inappropriate than ever in that setting. The fog was being driven back over the highest ridge; what little escaped into the Bulito and the other canyons dissipated into the blue. I could see the fog piled up on itself the whole length of the coastal ridges.

That day the light sparkled. Everyone was gone from the ranch, and the beach had become wild again. So little time is needed for a beach to return to its normal self once people leave.

At the breakwater, all was silenced; the offshore wind was checked by the high bluffs, creating a dead calm in the ocean beyond. The place was cozy, sunny, and still. Sea lions, as curious as always, rode the breakers close by. More of them had congregated that day in the calm. The sea was a shimmering light blue, and the plus tide had marked its limit with a small, sharp sand ledge at the cove. One sea lion swam toward us in the foam of the breakers, his dark body showing in the rise of the waves, his shining, egg-shaped head pointing straight at us, viewing us closer and closer, but silently. I found myself trying to establish the seal's pointed head in my mind's eye for identification. The prehistoric cave artists must have done just that. They had drawn single lines to convey an animal's most telling characteristic, especially its most typical stance, as well as its barely suggested outline seen at a distance.

The cave artists' fine delineations had conveyed the memories laid down in their minds by experiences repeated countless times. Now, in later life, I was trying to put into words similar lines of experience, distillations of communicating shapes and colors imprinted through the years. I had cultivated a knack for seeing forms in childhood, when my twin and I were at our most sensitive and impressionable stage. A wild animal would never stay in sight more than a minimum of time, so we learned to register it in a split second. In fact, more often than not an animal's unique flight pattern was the best identification of its species. I know of no one with this facility who has not lived much of his life, especially his young life, in the wilderness. Old-time cattlemen on the job especially depended on this ability to identify animals quickly in the most inaccessible places. A characteristic movement, a smudge of color, the twitch of an ear, or the switch of a tail was all they had to depend on.

Prehistoric people, it seems, used these same identifying lines and forms not only for detection but also to convey their deepest feelings. A single line on a cave wall could communicate the depths of what the artist felt for the great predators and the game. Archaeological experts claim that prehistoric paintings were scratched in the stone cave walls as part of ritual, which is why so many drawings overlap. But I found myself "overlapping" when trying to articulate what I saw or felt or thought or sensed from my horse's back on these trips. I struggled again and again over my choice of words for the sake of meaning and the satisfaction it gave me. The pressing need to deal with the threats in my life also accounted for my using so much repetition in my thinking, saying "it" over and over, this way, that way, and in all the myriads of possible ways. My thoughts were as repetitive as prayer rituals.

Primitive man and woman had to adjust to their dangerous environment as best they could. [Women are now thought to have been the cave-painting artists because the artists' handprints and footprints are so small—see Buffie Johnson, Lady of the Beasts (San Francisco: Harper Religious Books, 1988), 62.] Their worship of the animals and repeated depiction of them certainly was part of this effort. Modern man and woman must have the same need to feel awe and respect for what is beyond them. But the question is, what does the wild animal hold for us now, when its potency has been subdued and it is not even an economic necessity? Does the wild animal, by any chance, hold open the only small door left to the magic of life, to the substratum of our living, from where our own religion comes? I think so.

Ancient peoples, it is said, looked upon the animals as their ancestors; perhaps we have to do the same to regain our sanity in our modern, hostile, asphalt-and-steel environment, where we repress our natural spontaneity. At any rate, that was what I was doing for myself on my rides.

The beach sand was swollen with moisture from the roused tides; the hard, worn effect of summer had gone. The kelp was extensive, more so than usual, and may have served to keep the sea quiet. One blue heron stood far out on the kelp, looking at his feet in a concentrated way. He was fishing. The sun, sparkling on the mounting breakers, was almost blinding. Another sea lion, black and shining wet at the breakwater, was as curious as the other one—or perhaps he was the other one, caught up with us. Each time he submerged, he pulled his head into the water in a straight line, neck first, snout following. His long whiskers shone in the sun. Sinking into the water as a human bather would, he would then hump himself over and down in order to dive. There was a third seal, too; they must have been fishing in that quiet, sunlit water.

Examining my scribbled notes between visits was making me realize that I was gaining satisfaction apart from the pleasure of recording the immediate effect of the place. I was "unloading" my accumulation of impressions and reflections gathered in the between times. In the process, I was getting a feeling of well-being and satisfaction on a larger scale, as happens to the artist or scientist who is compelled to create. That the creative act could bring about stability was not a new idea. But I was finding out firsthand what others knew and had experienced. One inevitably repeats patterns of life. The difference is that each person's expression is tied in with a specific childhood environment and a unique personality, as well as the times. In the last analysis, creativity is not concerned with what is new, except in details. To think of oneself as original would be megalomaniacal and dishonest. Rediscovering what has been known all along, but carries one's own stamp, is a personal contribution. At least I told myself so.

One might say that creativity is a process of sounding for the eternal patterns of life, the eternal elements within one—the instincts, perhaps—and then applying one's own individuality to shape them accordingly. There are so many interlocking factors involved. In searching and straining for the single telling line or the abstraction or the fitting word, one does have a chance of touching on what is unique to this one person.

Prehistoric art is so impersonal that it is tempting to think there was no artist involved. Did the conformity of animals cast such a spell on the artists that they could not stray from the typical wild movements and gestures, so uniform that the animals depicted are easily recognized to this day? This sameness does not make wilderness monotonous. In fact, experience proves quite otherwise, for no matter how often the reality of the wilderness is expressed, its uniqueness shows through. A vital message improves with repetition in the same way rituals and ceremonies develop with use. And, paradoxically, there is only one of everything.

Prehistoric art—whether the subject is right side up, vertical, whole, in part, or superimposed—carries a message of purity of line, of vitality, of infinite power. Most striking is the sensitivity and acute perception of the artist, whose observation captures the power of the animal. Those earliest paintings, I believe, were done from the level of the animal within the primitive artist, making them almost self-portraits—another indication of the artists' being female. The artist saw herself in the animal, if not the animal in her. The few times humans appear in these paintings, they are given as stick figures such as small children draw.

We are used to hearing how important it is to express ourselves lest we dry up or become destructive. Like us, the primitive cave painters must have been painting their prayers for guidance, for stability perhaps. How much was all that praying to themselves in animal forms similar to the efforts of our modern believers, who have lost faith in their guiding institutions and are now having to find their guidance inside themselves? It seems to me that it is important to make the effort to create, because if one creates something that surpasses one's ordinariness, it is like finding something bigger than oneself from within. Wilderness does this for us, if we let it.

We were already well up into Sacate Canyon when I thought of the Naskapi Indian and how he found within himself what he called the "Great Man." These Labrador Indians were so isolated and so separated from one another by their environment that they developed individual circular designs representing the Great Man for each man. Each Indian's individual design was woven onto his pouch, in which he carried his most treasured possessions. It was this innovative act that held him, as an individual Indian, in constant contact with his inner self. For the lonely Indian, the Great Man in design became his religious symbol, his god. Naskapi Indians had none of the gathering places common to people who live in groups; each person had to carry his church and his god with him. In a way, modern people who have dropped out of organized belief have to find within themselves a similar focus. In order to find stability, many of us have to discover our Great Man or Great Woman and give him or her a chance to come into our individual lives. Internalizing what formerly had been "out there," whether animal or essence or power or creativity can feel like an audacity or a taboo. It is no wonder that an awkward feeling of shame or guilt can accompany such a process.

The more I thought about these issues, and the more I tried to express them, the less guilty I felt for being so preoccupied with this coastline. The lessening of guilt seems to be in proportion to my acceptance of the coast not only as a thing in itself but as a constellation of my imagination. Going back to the home of my childhood, where so much of me was buried, was beginning to feel legitimate.

Specialists tell us that the part of the brain that copes with memories of recent events atrophies in old people, freeing the part of the brain that is concerned with the past. It is hard to see why old age would cause one part of the brain to atrophy and not another. It seems likely that the physical needs urgent in old age would influence the brain selectively, enhancing parts of it and discouraging others—and, in the process, that the truth of one self that lies in the place of the past would come clear. At any rate, these thoughts fit nicely with my preoccupation with the coast that day.

Later, in my home in the north, I thought more about the cave paintings. Prehistoric artists may also have made their beautiful line drawings in the dark of the caves out of necessity. They must have gone inward in an outward way just by entering their caves. It seems to me that they were painting invocations. Each line in each drawing was a recognition of the importance of animals. The animals were both their source of nourishment and their gods, who sometimes needed to be placated or appeased or persuaded to help in times of trouble. This art could have eased the leaden feeling that comes with the hardships of daily existence.

At least that was my experience. I was finding a surprising release from reviewing my ranch notes, which revived ranch scenes by means of crucial trigger words. As I noted earlier, I was, in a sense, painting with lines as brief and accurate as wits would allow. The crudity of expression kept alive the freshness of the experience.

In my reading, I came upon Wilhelm Worringer's thesis "Abstraction & Empathy," written in 1908 about cave paintings. Worringer described the paintings as instinctive works created without intervention by the intellect. He suggested that the cave artists' urge for abstraction arose from a need to externalize the objects of their world, thus divesting them of their "caprice and obscurity in the world picture" and making them less threatening. This thought is mirrored in S. Giedion's comment that cave art originated in "cosmic anguish." These statements, in a vague way, brought into relief a little of what I was reaching for.

On that day in the Sacate, in the deepest sense I had made the most of everything around me. The emphasis on the moment, the imminence of everything from objects to inner feelings, and the heightening of my childhood environment had all created something of a journey of discovery. I had also felt a bit of the rescue of my sense of the eternal, which lay buried in childhood, or, perhaps, overlaid it.

Using my psychological knowledge, I was trying to understand why I would always dream of the ranch when I was away from it. I would make many fine interpretations, satisfying a kind of intellectual hunger, yet the dreams would continue on and on, repeating the same themes and taking place in the same scenes. That should have been the tip-off, but I was slow to understand what the dreams were really about. When I finally had an opportunity to put my energies into the land—first by joining the family enterprise and later by means of the rides, the notes, and the expansion of the notes—an inner secret slowly revealed itself. Only then did the dreams cease. The need for the dreams and the messages they were pushing into my awareness at last could cease.

In writing out of my spontaneity, I was finding that the importance of the ranches in their physical reality receded. To me, this showed the existence of the greater force of an inner content. Reality was psychologically important only as the container of psychic substance. Finally, after sixty years, I was discovering that the psychic life *is* one's reality. Later, in my eighties, I would know that my inner life mattered more than the outer world. To this day, the few dreams I have that suggest the ranch are never specific, even when I am away from the ranch.

On my way up the Sacate that autumn day in 1964, paralleling its creek, I saw two covies of quail drinking in a nearly stagnant pool. So little water was left. The lack of water undoubtedly explained why there was so little wildlife in the fall. One small phoebe, somersaulting for insects, and an occasional flicker's red blur disappearing through the tops of the trees, drew my attention.

At the great rock ledge I looked for the monkey-faced owl that I had seen roosting there so many times—or his descendants. On this dark northern side of the canyon was a shallow cave cut across by a thin sandstone ledge, which formed an ideal perch that protected the owl from the road. Expecting to see him, I rode up the bank. And there he was: a beige creature with a wide, white, heart-shaped face and black eyes. His head swiveled over his back to look at me. His long, white legs, white front, and soft, beige back gave off a cleanliness that contrasted with the surrounding stains of his excrement.

The ranch was fading into fall; it was growing pale and diminished, but not blotted out as happens in the snow country. My horse and I finally climbed over the western ridge to the gate at the top of the Santa Anita. At the gate, I decided to go the long way home, by way of the highest ridge and then down into Bulito Canyon. I was experiencing a remembered confident childhood feeling—a sense that I could ride forever. Just then, Hollywood perked up, apparently at the thought of going home. He and I were making a whole. At each stop, when I dismounted he turned and butted me in the shoulder with his nose.

In the Bulito, anything that could be measured or described or abstracted was there: death, gentleness, delicacy, darkness, light, stillness, heat, and cold. All could be savored, thanks to my horse's cooperation and even in spite of his irritating ways. Over all were the huge, impersonal silence, the color and the no-color, the clean dirt and the dust, which was just as clean, the roaring wind in exposed places, and the end of the year's dead sage; best of all was my pleasure in all this. My knees would not bend, but that was unimportant.

As I rode down into the canyon, I was glad to be alive. Artists have always known about beauty. I was only just then seeing it, really seeing it. The Indians spoke of the "thinking heart"; that was what I was doing, thinking in beauty, living in beauty. Riding down that beautiful canyon in the primeval setting, I felt myself lifted to an impersonal level, making me somehow right with my surroundings. It was an impersonality that belonged to my age, an aspect of the Chinese Tao. It was neither left nor right but above and below, away from the human struggle in the area of understanding and the field of meaning. In other words, the moment was for me momentous and privileged.

17

THE CLOUD

~ JANE ~

January 1987. If the temperature had not been below freezing at 3:30 this morning at Tepitates, where we have only kerosene lamps that are complicated to light, I would have written a book-length account of the meaning of the notes I had written in late 1964. I had reviewed them yesterday, and in my half-awake state this early morning, reams had wanted to be written. Now, after sleeping on "it" for the rest of the night, I find it almost impossible to recall what had been revealed, or to remember the "conclusions" that had followed. The cold light of day of rationality does not help! In the night, I had known I was at the source of an outpouring of half-conscious thoughts or reactions or impressions having to do with what has been happening all these years. However, the thoughts, or whatever they were, like the wildlife around us in the night, disappeared as day dawned, leaving only their tracks.

The notes that I felt could have caused this "revelation" related to a strange experience in which I had become lost in a cloud while riding alone on the ranch some twenty years before.

~

October 1964. Monarch butterflies were everywhere. The fresh, young lupine and the young sage were strong and vigorous, and in the upper Bulito, thanks to a lot of rain, water was heard flowing once more. Around the old reservoir, meadowlarks laid down a soft, rich carpet of sound in the atmosphere, which was as solid as the clover and the grass. Crows' caws resounded, softly enough, but the meadowlarks predominated; the silence was part of them all.

An atmosphere of waiting prevailed; but waiting for what? Perhaps there would be another gentle rain, although there had already been enough. The green was so vivid in its reflection of the sun that it made me squint. Soon the spasm of fear that had come from the nightmare in the night left me. Imagine! A fear of horses! Never! But the dream horse had been about as large as the legendary Trojan horse!

And then, as though to fit in with the dream, I had gone to saddle my big, white horse, White Sides. (He had been called Silver when we bought him, but his name had annoyed me, so I had renamed him.) He was covered with dirt. The men at the barn said it looked as if he had been rolling in the mud; he had messed himself up beyond use. That was one on me, from the look in his eyes, but I fooled him; we would go out no matter how dirty he was. This time we put on the hackamore; it was easier on him, so he did not throw his head and fuss, as he did with the bit. We did not know then that White Sides had been broken only to a hackamore.

January, months ago, had already conveyed the message: clover year. Clover always returns to fix nitrogen in ground that has been used up by the grass. Filaree was there, too, at the tip-top of the Bulito. There was so much of it on the eastern side of the ridge, overlooking the houses below, that our hoof sounds were muffled in the thick turf. Up there, the breakers seemed surprisingly near; I wondered whether sound rises, as heat appears to do when it is replaced by cold air. Point Conception stood out, as did the San Miguel, Santa Rosa, and Santa Cruz islands. They were as visible as the ocean sounds were clear. But there was a heavy, low fog coming toward us from the ocean.

The early calves amused me; their saucy curiosity suited the feeling that spring was on the way. Cavorting in the green grass, they looked positively brand-new; I was pleasure-bound, too, I thought. A largish, orange-yellow bird with black markings more or less like stripes showed up in the right fork of the Bulito. It was hot and still on the road, which paralleled the property-line fence at the back. Cattle seemed to have camped there; the grass had been eaten down near the catch-dam, just short of the stiff gate that opened into the San Julian, the neighboring ranch. Right there at the head of our Santa Anita Canyon, which almost joined the Bulito, stood nine deer, one buck among them. They were gray in color, a proof of good condition.

Traversing the top of the Bulito's eastern hill, I became uncertain whether I was dealing with fog or mist or clouds. Whatever it was, white billows of it soon poured into the canyon from the south on a rain wind. Like a ground fog, it filled the canyon as water fills a ditch. Then everything was blanked out by the mist around us. The dense fog made the noise of the breakers seem close, yet there was no longer even a glimpse of the ocean; a foghorn was blowing full blast. The wind was gentle and not cold, yet persistent. Everything ordinarily visible was under wraps; I could see ahead barely a few yards. It was all very strange.

Slowed down, I had time to think. That day, I had not felt a need to ride for my own well-being. I had had a long, deep sleep and was feeling in good shape. I wondered, then, whether my rides were another form of deep sleep—in a way, one and the same thing. In a vague sense, it was true that levels of my daytime life insinuated themselves into my awareness during these rides. These "riding thoughts" did not come from a place as deep as the dream level, but from deep enough. Were the dream horse and the symbol of sleep perhaps the same? But then, what about the horse's also being the symbol of death? And then I remembered my nightmare. Could one say from all this that sleep, especially deep sleep, was a small death, a nightly reminder of what is inevitable? Perhaps, then, death was not something to worry about.

So perhaps it was the deep sleep that lessened the poignancy of this ride. The country had indeed lost its magic that day. Still, I was very glad to be there, in spite of not being able to invoke much imagination.

I continued on my dirty white horse into the Bulito's right fork until we were pushed back by rocks and the stiff scrub sage. The terrain also descended steeply, ending somewhere down in the fog-mist, which was still thickening. It was too difficult for a horse. The day was darkening, making me wonder whether we should go back while we had the fence to guide us. Yet we pushed on.

Despite the threatening mist, I decided to try an old trail up onto the highest ridge dominating the left fork, which made up our northern boundary. In a burst of energy, my horse got us up there. The effort, the actual climbing, gave me an airy feeling of altitude, especially when we could overlook the southern ridge. Proof that the trail was unfrequented came when a large deer sprang out almost from under us. He must have been resting, judging from the presence of a neat, round place in the tall, rough grass that resembled a large nest. We surprised him so much that he crashed through a thicket of dead stuff in his wild scramble to get out of our way.

Further on, we came to some tall tanbark oaks marking the highest point on the ranch, at the edge of the botanical relic area. The wind sounding through them suggested a forest. Coyote signs were everywhere along the overgrown road. Behind me, the fog was still barreling into the upper reaches of the canyon, piling up in cold, dense, gray mists.

Slowly, after I got over my ambivalence about riding at all that day, I began to feel part of the place. The cold, blinding, cloud-like mist, the adventure, the wildness, and the effort finally brought my imagination to life. Strange: only then did I remember waking that early morning with another odd dream. In it, I had been walking along an unknown road. A huge, black cloud, blinding me, had blotted me out; then, finally, for no apparent reason, it had cleared away. That was all. In the night, it had been a black cloud; now, in daytime, the cloud was gray, almost white, but still cutting off all vision. It was utterly impossible to see ahead more than a few yards, in both dream and reality.

A coyote with unusually broad ears loped away, totally at ease. There was hardly any wildness in him. He must have been just out of sight, paralleling us, as coyotes often do. This one's shape was squarer than usual, and his coat was more yellow than brown.

The mist drifted in, feeling more and more like a wet blanket. It was cold and still blinding. Again I wondered whether I should turn back and take the longer road home, since it was getting late. Yet something made me keep going.

We followed the fence line on the northern boundary, where faint tracks of some vehicle showed. The tracks suggested a way out, but by then the cloud-mist had become so thick that nothing was familiar. My "bought" horse, not knowing the terrain, was no help. He could not smell his way out, nor did he have the instinct to do so if he could. Horses are as easily dulled in their wits as humans if they have no experience of wilderness.

A great hawk flew right over our heads, moving as swift as a bullet through the cloud. Because of his silent concentration, I knew he was hunting. But how could the hawk see better than I? I followed what looked like bulldozer tracks. I thought they might have been made while working on a firebreak and just might also indicate a road. I did not dare leave the fence; I kept it in my view for safety. Another hawk flew over our heads, so close I could have touched him. He also was hunting. Perhaps so dense a mist blinds wild prey so that they cannot see the predator until it is on them. I wondered how the hawk could keep from smashing into something, but then I decided that all wild things must be integral parts of their ecology. The hawks must know exactly where they are and what the obstacles might be, and their victims must be fittingly vulnerable.

Several times, but only after identifying place marks to get me back to the fence, I rode out looking for a trail that might take us back to the canyon. Finding nothing, I had to return to the bulldozer tracks. They led us down, deep into a wild grove of oaks. The descent was so precipitous that I had to lead my horse, only to come to a sudden stop at a descending wall of rough rocks too steep for either of us. We had to retrace our way by means of the horse's hoofprints.

Finally, we came to an apparently unused gate. On the post a cow's skull was barely visible, its long, sweeping horns pointing into the sky. The eerie effect was exaggerated by the mist, which closed in, denser than ever. The gate, tied up with bits of wire, was obviously neglected; cattle would not like it here. It took forever to untangle the wire and pass through, only to have to put the gate in place again. By then the heavy mist had aggressively, totally cut off our outlook.

Across the fence everything was unfamiliar, though I felt sure we must be on the neighboring ranch, the San Julian. The ground cover, a short, impenetrable chaparral, did not resemble anything I had seen in the Bulito. But there were tracks that apparently would take us down the other side of the ridge, in a direction away from home. We pushed on, having spent more than an hour looking for a way out.

Without warning, a used road presented itself. As we followed it, the cloud suddenly dissipated, showing us that we were not far from the head of the Bulito. From then on the going was easy, made especially so by a reasonable gate separating the two ranches.

Weeks later, I thought more about this trip. The dream of being lost in a black cloud, followed by the actual experience of being lost in a white one, made me wonder. Had that day's happening already been in the cards? Why a black cloud as symbol and a white one in reality? I had already experienced the cloud in my sleep, so the worry during the waking episode had been mitigated. I wondered whether one always experienced reality in this way. That is, was experience always either softened or exacerbated by what happened in the night? I had always thought that experience took place either in sleep, on a deep, subliminal level, or in the daytime, as an actual happening, but not both. Apparently I was wrong, and this may explain why my being lost for so long had not been so frightening.

Finally, I concluded that everything in our lives must be preordained, predestined—that all the details of living were already known, but visible only to those who could somehow lift themselves out of time. In a way, it was a reassuring thought. It took away, for a moment, feelings of responsibility for myself and, best of all, for my part in the loss of our ranches. Jung would have called this happening archetypal because of its coincidental psychic and physical aspects, in which inner and outer events synchronize.

Weeks later still, I remembered that before being lost in that cloud, I had had no sense of direction. I had seemed to be floating; there was an unreality around me. Slowly it dawned on me that I had been "in a cloud" figuratively. It had been one of those times in life when little makes sense, when everything is flat and gray and unimportant—times when one can only give in and wait for the energies and concentration and inspiration to return. So that was it. I had been given a warning of what was to come: a spell of feeling lost, a time of not knowing, until the cloud lifts of itself and life can continue in its usual way. I would have to wait for more understanding, which would come many months later. It was nothing startling in the way of conclusion, perhaps; yet, in the sense of what predetermination implied, it seemed an extraordinary statement, affecting me totally. No small potatoes.

Now, more than twenty years later, in January 1987 in Tepitates, I lay awake after a momentous revelation that felt like an archetype, with not only its image surfacing but also its content; and I, the dreamer, was surrounded by the reality of wilderness. I asked myself a simple question: Why do I have so much need to work on these ranch notes? Had I been in civilization, with a good light over my bed, I would have worked on the pages until I fell asleep again. Fortunately, I had instead to wonder about the urge.

Immediately I "knew" that my work on these papers was for my benefit, that the Self, my psyche as a whole, needed to speak and thereby also find for my ego its (her) right place in the Self's scheme. The writing would somehow explain that I was honoring an archetypal psychic totality—something vastly bigger than "me" in me. This part of me had recently begun functioning again as, in my eighties, I worked to edit the material first written more than twenty years earlier. My whole psyche, containing my ego center of consciousness, was being revealed in the night as a phenomenon actually corresponding to the totality of the ranch. It was the archetype itself, not its image, that could not live in the light of day. For a long time I had suspected as much; but that night, the how and why that came to me, in the language of the deepest psychic reality, confirmed my suspicion.

The actual phenomenon of the archetype of the Self, its subjective inner aspect and its outer, physical aspect, namely, the actual wilderness around our house, which had declared itself in the night as its substantive self, would not stand scrutiny. I felt, however, that the nighttime message also implied that the connection between the ranch and the telling of the story of this inner-outer alliance had been verified; this nighttime revelation was the proof.

The words that had surfaced in the night, at other times during the writing of these notes, and during the present editing had never been "mine," really. They had come from an impersonal source that had its own laws. In fact, the actual words could have been the point where the inner and outer totalities met. If this was the case, the previous night's experience had to have an archetypal meaning. In my half-sleep, I had known it to be so. In the dark early hours, in my mind's eye, I had made a diagram to remind myself in the morning what had been revealed. It is reproduced here.

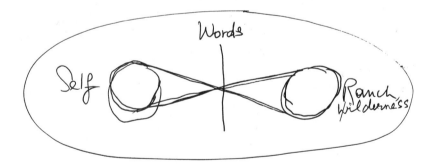

Where the lines cross is where the words stand and where the meaning concentrates. (In the night, the word "adjunct" for where the lines cross came to me forcibly, but I do not understand how it applies.

Perhaps inner and outer enhance each other where they join.) The left circle refers to the subjective, the inner psychic totality, and the right circle refers to the outer, or physical, totality. The diagram shows the principle of the thunderbolt, a symbol of power (among other things) in Tantric Buddhism, where it is called *vajra*, or *dorje* in Tibetan.

As I reflected, I realized more fully than before that I had been raised from the age of four in a situation of power and meaning and that the whole of the ranch had touched me in a drastic way, as it had the others who lived there. And, with luck, it seemed that I might understand in my old age what had happened.

Writing about the night's adventure comes hard. If only one could recover the wealth of understanding that sometimes happens in one's sleep!

This perception of the touching of inner and outer totalities may be as common as people are numerous. For example, an individual who does not experience wilderness could experience the same meeting of inner dream life and outer surroundings if he or she continues in the house in which he or she grew up. What is rare is to discover that one's inner self also needs what is outside in order to come to fruition—that the midpoint is also where the creative drive and impulse happen. But there must be a balance: there can be neither a dominating ego nor an overpowering outer condition.

I believe that in my life on the ranch my horse equalized the ranch's overpowering effect by being an extension of my ego. The horse obeyed my commands, but he also took me to places I could never have managed on foot. He made it possible to experience in broad outlines a whole territory, to survey the entire outer, self-regulating phenomenon known as wilderness. On those trips over the ranch, my horse was instinct, mobility, power, and rhythm. The support he provided invited my insides to speak, to help me react to the beauty and to compound it with joy and the urge to tell about it. Without a horse strengthening my ego in the face of the overpowering outer circumstance, this might never have happened.

But the most important question is still unanswered: Were we, as children, dwarfed by the bigness of the land and its total lack of ego? Is that why country people tend to be shy? Ego, as far as I can see, is not part of country people's arsenal, especially in their dealings with others. I wonder whether the Self-as-wilderness invaded us too young. Did it draw out prematurely the power and reality of our inner selves, to the detriment of ego development and with a consequent inability to adapt to civilization, where the ego is highly developed? Perhaps I was finding that there is, in old age, time to make up for those early years, even though one's creativity might not ripen for others to see until then. I wonder whether the result might be all the richer for waiting; perhaps, too, it may not matter if the expression goes unnoticed.

I believe I gravitate to these notes to get myself "squared away" and to release some of the meaning and power that are generated between the inner and outer aspects of the Self where the lines of the diagram cross. This is my way to meditate.

The outpouring of thoughts on that January night must have put my ego in its right place, because I soon fell asleep. That in itself is proof of the rightness of the thoughts. For someone like me who is restless by nature, sleep is important, just as death is significant for anyone who questions life.

My experience of the release of this material may have been especially dramatic because throughout my writing I had recognized the self-regulating, totally self-sufficient, complete independence of the wilderness. I had seen how people who enter the wilderness must obey the laws of nature or else destroy it or be destroyed. I knew by then that if wilderness is respected, it can create an ambiance for better living. It can help with one's self-completion through the realization that only as one honors what is bigger and greater and more potent than oneself can one be normal. I have witnessed how troubled people of any age sooner or later find their self-respect if they abide by nature's physical laws and the overtones of wilderness values.

In thinking over my night experience, I understood more clearly why so many members of my family and those who worked on the ranch found that they could not leave—or if they did leave, that the ranch haunted them, sometimes consciously, sometimes not. I understood better why some would destroy the place in an effort to free themselves of a tie they did not acknowledge. I had to return in old age to find out why I had bought back a hundred acres overlooking the Chumash Indian burial ground and Point Conception, which is known by Indians across our continent as their Western Gate, their staging area to the other world.

18

WILDERNESS AND THE SACRED

~ LYNDA ~

My mother describes her awe at the way the wilderness stirs her and draws her into a meditation. As she recalls this effect, she comes to understand that putting words to it is a profound experience, a conscious experience of the sacred.

Over long years that have passed since I lived immersed in the ranch wilderness, I have found that I feel much the same way in my connection with wilderness wherever I find it. Making this discovery took most of my life, and in reflecting on it now, I can see that I was drawn to the discovery by an "impersonal source," as my mother describes it.

In spite of, or perhaps because of, my difficulty in finding my way into ranch life, the ranch became my matrix, as iron ore is the matrix of iron. Its existence is still essential in my life, even though I am rarely there. For twenty years after I left the ranch to be married, I persuaded myself that I had no interest in it, no need of its resources; the city was enough. For twenty years, I built a life with a great piece missing from its foundation, and the day came when I had to start filling the gap.

Since then, I have undertaken to emerge from that matrix; but unlike iron and its matrix, I will probably never separate from it. My effort is only to differentiate myself from it, to discover how my experience of that wilderness prompts me, frightens me, enlightens me.

The land my husband, Klaus, and I acquired in the Sierra Nevada foothills was about half an hour's drive from Placerville in the gold country. Most of that half hour of driving was over country road; then there was another mile or so on an old dirt logging road. We had eighty-five acres, but because our property shared a boundary with the Eldorado National Forest it seemed limitless, plugged into the wilderness.

The American River lay several hundred feet below our southern border, and our porch overlooked it. There was a neighbor a quarter of a mile away in one direction and another neighbor a quarter of a mile away in the other direction. The terrain was rolling, with pines and manzanita and grass that turned golden in summer.

The land was undeveloped and unmarked by humans, except for signs of logging from forty years back, and placer mining eighty-five years before that. We found an ancient ore car, shovels, and square nails in a ravine near where we put our cabin. Over the years, I reopened the old "miners' ditch," as the miners' aqueduct was locally known; it had been totally overgrown. This aqueduct had brought in the water necessary to run the placers, which pulverized the ore with forceful streams of water to wash out the gold.

The "ditch" traversed our property and went on into the national forest, and it became my path into the wilderness. After about three miles, it stopped in a ravine where there was a substantial little river. I made that ravine my destination on my excursions. I would sit there and ruminate, watching for the red salamanders who raised their families under the rocks. I would face upriver, watching as the water dropped down toward my salamander pool over rocks and rotten logs, making the air fresh with a series of small falls. After a while, I would get up and head back along my path toward home.

We had acquired Juno, our third German shepherd, a couple of months before we found this property, and Juno became instrumental in my understanding of myself as embedded in the wilderness. In this setting, with Juno, I learned, more or less consciously, to merge with "the animal." Sitting by the river pool in the forest, I would watch Juno march into its center and sit down so that only her head and neck were above water. She would lap and bite the water, watch the skaters skim the surface, prick her ears at salamanders, and snap at mosquitos. She was immersed in her environment, one with it; watching her, I could feel the same.

Somehow, having Juno as my mediator, I could experience unity with nature and at the same time know my disjunction from it. The clearer I was about being different from Juno, the more deeply I dared merge with her and nature.

Klaus and I took Placerville for granted for most of our fifteen-year sojourn there. But when we decided to move to Maine, I awakened to the knowledge of what our Sierra property meant to me. It was as if the property were a screen through which I had to reach to find the true matrix that was the ranch, glimmering limitless beyond. It is the ranch that is my link to my origins. As Placerville and Juno had linked me to the ranch and to my animal instincts, so do the images of the ranch and of all animals link me to my sense of what really matters.

Realizing how utterly I had entered into life in the gold country brought home to me what I had previously denied: I was as much a ranch creature as I had ever been. I had never really left the ranch. In fact, my not realizing the strength of my bond with the ranch had kept me from expressing my feelings about it. Only as I came to know my experience consciously could I extricate enough interest and enthusiasm to transform my experience of life from inarticulate subjectivity to more communicative forms. The ranch had me in thrall, and I needed to know it. It will always have me in thrall, but I am no longer submerged. Now I can reflect on it, and draw from my experience of it, in my effort to articulate my thoughts and feelings.

Being "in thrall" is a primitive form of religious experience. The joy of swinging up onto a horse in the freshness of the new day as I headed out to round up cattle on the ranch was an example of that. I felt tremendous enthusiasm—which means, literally, being "filled with

God"—inspired by the clear air, the lively horse, the vast setting, and the prospect of an enjoyable job to do. I was part of something bigger than I am and had no wish to escape it. It was a completely solitary state; I told no one how I felt.

For people throughout history, the image of God has elicited awe as a symbol of ultimate potential and infinite meaning. But I grew up without organized religion or mention of God, so I turned to wilderness and nature instead. As a result, I had no language for my experience and no form of ritual or group ceremony by which to relate to what moved me. I remained in a primitive state of enthrallment.

It seems to me, though, that had I had "God" and an organized way of relating to God, I still would have needed a physical manifestation to give me an active connection with the sacred. For me, the wilderness, and especially the ranch in its overarching power, embodies the sacred, awe-inspiring source from which comes the reason to live and create.

As I understand it, what is meant by God and religion is an encompassing container and reference source larger than we are, which helps us bear the overwhelmingness of infinity. Something, someone, is in charge; there is order in the apparent chaos; there is continuity in spite of our fragility. We will wake up tomorrow to another sunrise. In the absence of God and religion, I turned to nature, seeking its regularity and predictability while being frightened by its infinity and unpredictability. At the same time, I was sustained by the palpability of that which overwhelmed me; I could touch, taste, hear, and smell the natural world.

I think that the great intuition that is God and religion must periodically be refreshed by the physical, and that may be why there are periodic incarnations, physical miracles, and crises of faith. The wilderness, both as an idea and as a concrete reality, may be necessary to help balance the vast abstraction of religious imagery. Wilderness is big enough for the job of incarnation.

It has the necessary attributes. It has infinite complexity of form and color; its cycles have neither beginnings nor endings; species come and go (even without the participation of humans): the wilderness is never the same. Nature extends backward in history through the time of our ancestors to early man and before. Even without thinking about it, we all know that we came from the darkness of time. The true beginning of us all is mythical, infinite—when did humans begin? No one really knows. Our apparently infinite history is as awe inspiring as our potentially infinite future. This awe is triggered by contact with what we feel to be sacred. Life and infinity are sacred.

The wilderness can provide us with a continuing contact with life and infinity; it gives us the opportunity literally to seek our beginnings with no fear that such beginnings might turn out to be a single moment in time, thus finite and no longer compelling. We want to seek; the excitement is in the quest. We do not want it to end. Thus, the wilderness is a sacred place. It offers a quest that one can enter into body and soul.

There are many ways to seek one's destiny, enlightenment, and reason to live; some of them, such as dreams, theories, memories, and insights, are necessary guideposts in the wilderness experience. But the wilderness is perhaps the richest place for the body to participate in the quest. And without physical experience of the sacred, we can lose our way.

The quest is a sacred phenomenon having to do with our seeking the source of life, the source of our own personal lives, and the meaning of life in general. The quest is a more conscious form of enthrallment, also compelling but without the paralysis that can accompany primitive enthrallment. The quest can take many forms. I remember, as a child, searching for the perfect abalone shell on the beach and for arrowheads left by the Chumash Indians on the mesas. Both carried some unarticulated magic—the rainbow colors of the abalone brightened me, and the elegant triangle of the arrowhead gave me a surge of energy.

I found myself undertaking a new search in our gold country weekend place, perhaps as a continuation of the abalone shell quest. This time I sought the perfect crystal. Where gold is, or has been, there are crystals. Like the abalone, the crystal carries the magical properties of the rainbow and the power to transform light. I was keeping a journal during those years in the gold country in which I would record my experiences and discoveries. Time after time, I would note my crystal finds and catch myself spelling the word "christal." I knew at once that I was spelling the word wrong, but it took me a while longer to realize what was moving me to do so. The power of the search was the power of the Christ image. It was a sacred search for wholeness. For me, the meaning of Christ is the idea that the seeking of wholeness is a way of life, but, even as Christ was an imperfect manifestation of wholeness in his human form, so are we. The *image* of wholeness, however, gives us a lifeline for guidance and support while we fulfill our lives as completely as we can.

I never found a perfect crystal in all those years in the gold country. But, toward the end of our time there, I did find a wonderful one. It was good sized and smoky in color. It was a single shaft with a complete, four-sided pointed end and an uneven blunt end. It had several internal bubbles and other imperfections, and it was nicked on the outer surface. But it was all crystal, free of encumbrances of any kind. It was nearly perfect, so it brought my quest for crystals to an end.

One gain from my quest in the gold country was my coming to realize that I can sustain my link to life and the Self even though the ranch has been sold. My experience of the unknowable continues; my sense of the quest continues. For me, the infinite is now conjured up by certain physical settings. If I maintain my relation to any such setting, my relation to life and my feeling of regulation by the Self will be secure.

19

A Fox on the Rock

~ *Jane* ~

January 1987. In all my years on the ranch as a young person, I never knew the foxes. It was not until I was over sixty-five and had moved back to the ranch, fifteen hundred feet up in Tepitates, that I got to know them. (As previously noted, Tepitates means "A Sacred High Place" in the language of the Chumash.) Our house is in the foxes' territory, where the rocks and cliffs and chaparral make it impossible for people to intrude. The foxes, along with some coyotes and at least one cougar and her kittens, live on our ridge. Our hundred-acre parcel, strewn with sandstone boulders and penetrated by deep sandstone caves, is perfect for these wild creatures.

We moved into our house in the summer of 1975 and proceeded to settle down. We developed the habit of tossing all our kitchen scraps, except left-over tidbits, into the chaparral below us. We knew that the sun and animals and insects would finish them off in no time. The tidbits went into a dog's bowl outside the kitchen door. Getting ourselves installed and accustomed to the new set of circumstances took until the fall of that first year. Then we had to go back to work in Kentfield, California, in the San Francisco Bay Area, so the house was left on its own until the end of the year.

When we returned for our second stay, it was, for southern California, an early spring. Flowers were out; the sunny weather and lengthening days were giving the birds thoughts of mating. Everything was coming to life. It was a happy time, and we were soaking in the solitude, silence, and balmy atmosphere.

One late afternoon soon after our arrival, a pair of foxes came to visit. A big, reddish fellow and his mate, a demure, almost soft, yellow creature less than half his size, appeared on our kitchen terrace. Following them were five gray kits big enough to climb up and down the rock face there. Evidently in our first week there, we had been declared harmless.

The big male put himself at the top of the highest rock, from where he could see quite far. The mother of the brood sat on our bench. The young fry played chasing games, complete with mock fights and scampering in every direction. We watched through our glass kitchen door panel. When I threw a banana among them, the kits fought over it, rolling over each other and chasing and stalking the banana before finally digging into it with their teeth.

A visiting small dog was with us in the house that day. In curiosity, it came to the kitchen door. I saw the lady fox lower her muzzle and point it straight at the dog. Immediately, with no detectable sound, all five babies disappeared down a thin trail at the end of the terrace. The games were abruptly ended as the parent foxes stiffly followed the general exodus.

This show was only the beginning of many afternoons in the foxes' "play yard" that was our back terrace. We watched them with enormous pleasure. They became our constant subject of conversation with anyone who dropped in.

Once, when the whole family was there and each parent was strategically placed, all five kits grabbed hold of their mother and began to nurse. She walked laboriously among a seething mass of baby fur and slowly worked her way out of their reach.

Seeing what a large family she had, we bought canned dog food for her. More often than not, the male would beat her to the food and swallow it whole, or nearly whole. She would sit in the background, waiting. The first time this happened, I put out a second canful for her. She moved gracefully round and round it. She seemed hesitant. Thinking? Wondering? Or what? Then she took a smallish bite, held it in her jaws, looked around, and swallowed it. The second mouthful she held on to, firmly, and trotted off down the trail, obviously to distribute it among her kits. From the direction she took, their den must have been under a large boulder close by.

We were treated to these late-afternoon entertainments daily. At times the young ones would scrape against our kitchen door, possibly looking for more dog food. The following spring, the den was placed so far away that we never again saw baby foxes, but Mother and Father Fox still came regularly for handouts. When they could not resist the food and ate it on the spot, we rewarded them with double rations. The second lot of food was always taken away to their young.

Our salutation to each other in the days of our fox family was "There's a fox on the rock." In time it was shortened to "Fox on the rock."

Growing up on the ranch, we children all knew that there were many wild animals around us, but we rarely saw them. We always craved the sight of them, though, and were constantly on the alert. Invariably the sighting of one, being a rarity, would become the topic of the day.

Sighting an animal in the early days was much like receiving dream messages is for me now. The animals, like dreams, seemed to reveal themselves for a purpose. They appeared almost as part of our questing. Just as a dream never manifests beyond a minimum statement, the animals never overdid their revelations. If you do not strain for a dream just at the moment of its obliging, you will never learn its intent. Similarly, if we did not see the animal totally and for as long as possible, it was just too bad. The animals are there without our knowing, and they know more about the observer than the observer can ever know about them. It is the same with the dream that just barely comes out of the chaparral of the unconscious to let you know of its existence, especially when you have given up hope of dreaming.

The trouble with modern photography is that it traps the beauty and intimacy of animal life while squandering its meaning by photographic permanency and proliferations. There are many extraordinary animal photographs, but the mystery, the elusiveness, and the divine quality of the wild animal are lost in them. No longer do people have the experience that we did as children on the ranch, before photography revealed all. We no longer get our fleeting messages from the brief glimpse of wildness; now we see everything. In photographs, creatures big and small are stopped in their tracks and lifted out of their world. They are plagiarized; their authenticity and originality are gone. Without context, there is no meaning.

No longer do we look and look into the wild places day after day after day, to be rewarded, occasionally by a moment's glimpse of a beautiful wild creature in its most taut, alert, and curious state as it looks back at us. Photos take the place of our looking because they reveal every conceivable stance, state, and act. But just look at the pictures; what do you have? Yes, a remarkable photo. You wonder how it was possible, how it was done. The mechanics are what matter. But the message? None. That comes only in the wild, when the animal gives you permission and the laws of coincidence are functioning.

That's it: you have to let the wild reveal itself on its own say-so. The wild animal will deign to show itself when it is ready, when it has weighed the situation, this way and that way and its way. Like the dream messages or the wind or whatever belongs to the wild, the animal comes in its own time and place. Not yours. You never have control. The animal's choice controls you.

If you do not respect the wild, you will see nothing. Sometimes, even when you do approach the wild respectfully, the denizen still is not ready to show itself. That is the experience I know best: for days and days and days, nothing appears. Then, without reason or rational regard for one's desert—for God knows why—the coyote, the fox, the puma, or the bobcat will glide by within your sight for a matter of seconds. The fatalistic, timeless, spaceless happening comes when it will: not because of you. And that is what makes it so treasured. You know the animals are around—you have seen their tracks—but until they show themselves, you have not been given the right to see them in their own milieu.

The experiences of the observer and the observed, the time and place, the moment—all these within the wild—make one a part, a merged part, of the whole. The experience is a kind of total meeting. Everything comes together, and that is the meaning of the rarity of the experience. So many divergent, separate, incongruous factors are brought together when the wild creature deigns to appear. Curiosity in the creature, quite as much as the human's wish to see the animal, brings the two together. It is a convergence, in the same way that the appearance of the dream is a convergence with the dreamer. The observer, the dreamer, the creature, and the dream are all on the same path. Without wilderness and without the great inner psychic matrix, there are no such magical moments.

We need magic. The fantastic modern photography is ersatz by comparison. We become mechanical and soulless, we are robots, if we are without wilderness to verify humanity's inner wilderness.

What is true for the animal is also true for the wildflower. All of a sudden, after looking for days for a tulip in the sagebrush, for instance, there it is: full blown, lovely, perfect, its mottled lavender petals gleaming, almost mocking you in its superiority and glory and self-sufficiency. Yet the flower is just there, for the benefit of no one except perhaps the predator (deer, rabbit, or rat) that plucks it off its stem. A delicious morsel. No longer beauty in its own right, but an instantaneous part of the food chain.

Perhaps the greatest value of the wild is its purpose, aim, or objective. The song in its singing or the bloom at its maximum moment has no value other than its value of itself, to itself, in wilderness' terms. When wild creatures are transported for the sake of pleasure or money, their real essence vanishes; without context, the meaning is missing.

20

REMEMBERING

~ LYNDA ~

It is strange about remembering. As I relive times on the ranch, I gain the ranch in a new way. As the memories collect, it is as if a door opens on a grand scene. Since I became part of the scene very early in my life, I could not see it or even really know it while I was there. Remembering, I watch the scene emerge from the mist of symbiosis that was my embeddedness in the environment. Figures begin to move; faces come clear; I can almost feel the heat of the sun, smell the animals, taste the dust.

As a child, the only objective view I had of ranch life came in the distorted form of "cowboy movies." I loved going to see them in the suburbs, where my brother and I lived with our parents during the school year; movies were one of the boons of coming into civilization. But I was always disappointed afterward. Rarely did the movies capture the ranch reality as I knew it. They served the function of telling me what the ranch was not; it is only now, in remembering, that I begin to see what it was.

I do not know why I am surprised at the rewards of remembering; in psychology, the process is instrumental to healing. Remembering

165

demands acceptance of what was sad and painful about the past, but it also turns up what was good about it. In repressing the bad, we repress the good, too. So if the time comes when dissatisfaction with life demands it, remembering gives us back our pasts: in a boxful of photographs and letters, in conversation with family, or safely framed in the consulting room. There is an easing of tension we did not know we had, and a release of energy that had been absorbed in our effort to hold the past out of conscious awareness. As adults, we can tolerate experiences that might have overwhelmed or derailed us as children. The surprise is that good memories appear as well.

Symbiosis with the environment, such as my mother and I had with the ranch, has been called "participation mystique." In this form of symbiosis we become one with our settings—people, places, and animals. We are as unaware of ourselves in our settings as are tadpoles in a pond. Whether the situation is good or bad, we float in it; we know nothing else; our setting is our world. This phenomenon of symbiosis means we can pull in what we need to know through our senses, including the sixth sense known as intuition. Doing so sometimes gives us the best chance for survival.

For city children, this time of unself-consciousness is brief. By the time a city child is three or four, the disruption from this participation mystique has begun. Incredible stimulation toward consciousness, self-awareness, comes through television, street scenes, the many people, the absence of solitude, and the daily disappearance of working parents. Everyone is always going somewhere in the car: to the store, the doctor, the movies, the restaurant, on vacation. Opportunities to sink into one's own depths are rare; there is always someone around. For the city child, ego development is well under way by kindergarten.

On the ranch, symbiosis continued for my brother and me until we left to live in the north. I remember "discovering" mirrors when I was twelve or thirteen and trying to write a story about them. Mirrors give us self-awareness of a sort; we see some approximation of ourselves, but, more important, we begin to communicate consciously with ourselves. We posture and make faces; we watch our faces as we cry.

I remember seeing my sad face in the mirror the year I was fifteen. I was beginning to realize my personal existence as I lost my symbiosis with the ranch. I felt an ineffable sadness that year, though no particularly bad thing happened. I was coming to consciousness. Returning to the ranch each June after the long school year, I began to feel estranged, and it would take me days to find my way back in.

Yet, since it takes ego to be aware of Self, consciousness enriched my life in a new way. Being unaware of the Self, and submerged in it, as we were submerged in the ranch, meant harmony at some deep level, but there was no meaning. Meaning is not important to everyone, but for those who need it, symbiosis becomes a trap. My mother's experience of being trapped by her feelings for the ranch and of yearning to be reconnected with it is a case in point. Because both she and I were driven by some need to know ourselves more or less independently, we married urbane men and lived off the ranch. Other family members lived out their lives on the ranch; they did not seem to need to see themselves in the mirrors provided by civilization.

I wonder whether my grandmother and grandfather might have lived even longer had they not, in their eighties, moved into Santa Barbara and been forced to realize themselves in a new way. My parents, now in *their* eighties, spend most of their time on their small part of the ranch still. I can imagine that their life spans will be lengthened as a result, because I can see that the quality of their lives is enhanced.

The idea of mirroring as a way of knowing oneself is an important one in psychology. It begins in the mother's eye, as she gazes at her newborn baby and the baby sees her seeing. Growing up, the mirroring continues in the attitudes we feel that our families and peers have toward us. One of the wonderful advantages of having animals around is the unconditional love we receive from them. Our animals adore us whether we "deserve" it or not. We do not have to "earn our keep" with our animals, nor develop "communication skills." We have only to be with our animals.

The difference between mirroring by animals and mirroring by humans is the difference between being in the wilderness and being in the city. Animals and wilderness reflect the Self—no evaluation, just pure reflection. Humans and the city reflect the ego—plenty of evaluation and a distorted view of us, partly because we are misread and partly because we are afraid of being misread. In the wilderness, we are never misread. We are subject to the same natural laws as is every other entity, animate or inanimate.

Because I am remembering now, I am being rewarded with a new feeling of permanence in relation to the ranch. Because of these gathered memories, I can return to the ranch in my mind's eye and with a bodily resonance. I can hear my horse grunt as I tighten the cinch and the saddle creak as I climb onto his back. He humps a little as I settle in and as he accommodates to my weight. I rein him away from the other horses a bit and then watch the others get on their horses. Someone leads his horse across the main corral at the barn, where we have saddled up, in order to open the gate by the cattle guard. We ride through and stop for him to close the gate and mount up. Then we head off down the road toward whichever canyons we will be working that day. I can hear the clatter of hooves and the rasping of the crickets on the bridle bits, which give the horses something to play with in their mouths. I hear the early morning snorting and blowing of the horses as they settle down to the business at hand. And I watch everyone, noting how each one moves in the saddle to get the right fit, tugs his hat down so it will not blow off, sorts out the reins to ensure communication with his horse.

Most of the horses empty their bowels in the first few minutes, and I smell the fresh manure as it lies steaming in the dust. This phenomenon has always fascinated me; I wonder whether it has to do with preparing for action. Horses in movies seem not to do this; presumably it would offend the customers to show such a thing.

The great scene, opening up for me as I remember, always has at its center the horse-and-cattle part of our ranch life. For me, this realm was central. My mother describes the vegetative aspect of the ranch in fine detail, but I have only vague, impressionistic recall of that. I do remember the oaks everywhere, almost black-green, pronounced against the buff and gold of dust and summer grass. I also remember the eucalyptus trees, planted as windbreaks around the houses on the ranch long before I was born. But perhaps I remember trees because they moved. My mother's observation that my daughters appreciated most what moved applies to me, too. She thinks it has to do with youth, remembering her own childhood preference for what moved.

But my mother came to have to know about feed on the ranch when she took up the reins of ranch management in her middle age. Perhaps, in learning about the various grasses that made the best feed and hay for our cattle, she became aware of all the other growth—shrubs, flowers, trees—around her. I remember going out with Grandfather on horse-back or in the blue Jeep and watching as he would stop, get down, and check the wild oats to see if they had "headed out" yet. I felt, vaguely, that I should pay attention and learn about this myself, but I felt no need to do so. I was not responsible for ensuring the growth of the cattle and horses, only for doing my job as a "cowboy."

For me, animals, both domestic and wild, are vitally important. A large part of their fascination for me is their movement. I love to watch any animal move. On the ranch, I would fall into a hypnotic state during the cattle drives down the beach, partly from watching the cattle move along in their steady rhythm. Looking down at my horse's front feet, or at the feet of a horse near me, also always soothed and held me. Even now, the kinesthetic experience of my own movements, swaying slightly as my horse swings along in his big walk, gives me a reassuring sense of my own physical reality, as a Jacuzzi bath might for someone else. Walking in the wilderness or along the beach with a dog running free gives me a vicarious feeling of freedom in my body and soul.

I am really talking about the Self. The animal, in its thoroughgoing, instinctual way, is doing as it has always done: seeking its identity with the environment. It is guided by a force that transcends it; it follows a purpose that fulfills its design. It has no need of the negative modes that consciousness has brought us; it does not abuse or diminish or terrorize, except as those activities are part of survival. The animal may or may not seek power over others of its species, depending on the drives of that species. But it seeks this power in straight fights, leaving the vanquished in their places but rarely destroyed. If the vanquished animal is destroyed because of its wounds, or exile, or age, the survivor does not care. It is not relevant to him.

The principle of "eat or be eaten" results in death, but the intent served is survival, not power or self-enhancement for its own sake.

The animal has magical meaning for me. I am refreshed and renewed in watching an animal go about its ordinary way of life. I feel touched by the sacred and have a sense of the great scene we are all part of on this earth. The realization that there are so many individuals of all species, each a complete package of life, each following its path from birth to death, and all of us sharing our planet, strikes me with awe. I am full of the excitement of this awareness; truly our animal/human reality is divine. And the movement of each is what brings this reality home to me.

21

WHY DO I LIKE LIVING IN TEPITATES?

~ JANE ~

Much of what I have in my suburban home in Kentfield is missing here. The television reception is inadequate; the shows are poor; information is lacking. All the ease of living is also nonexistent.

What I do have in Tepitates is my integration with the process, the progress, and the cyclic verities of nature—especially the seasons. I am part of something so big that it carries me along, never mind the difficulties. I do not have to make my own decisions, other than choosing to stay here. Happy days for me mean a gentle, cool climate and a bright sun, monitored by the breezes and the fog and the cool of atmospheric forces. Best of all is the vegetation, which is never lost for good; it keeps its promise to return, no matter what the calamity.

This day, September 3, for instance, we are told by television that huge areas of the forestlands of the four Western states have burned because of a thousand lightning strikes on drought-dry vegetation. But today I can also say this: given less time than one might think, the vegetation will return, stronger and greener and more vital than ever. That is the great assurance that cyclic nature gives us.

At Tepitates, I can participate on a small scale in the enormous rhythm that is life and death. In Kentfield, I totally lose track of life's rhythms. The distracting interruptions and invasions of city life, so separated from the cyclic wheel of nature, throw me into all the deciding and choosing that are so tiring to the head.

Being carried along in Tepitates also may be, more than anything else, part of my progress toward a natural farewell to the biosphere. Here, living with what is so huge and so much greater than I am takes me normally and pleasantly to the prospect of my own personal demise. Death is here, too: in the present ending of the year and in the small deaths all around us that provide for the functioning of the food chain. Although death is a sadness if dwelled on, it is also an event in favor of further life, and so it is with the year's end.

Maybe my death will come to that, too. I like to think of myself as being part of the food-for-thought chain. Or, possibly, just the food chain; in some extended meaning, I can also accept that. My son, John, asked, when he located a boulder I could be buried under—one as big as a house—"Is this big enough?" In his mind, size has meaning. The boulder, in a sense, commemorates the greatness of natural life here; if I am to be even an inanimate part of it, how can I lose?

The hard side of life in Tepitates is scarcely noticeable, except for occasional spells of restlessness and of being too much alone, and the harshness of wind or cold or heat or rough terrain. And then there are the constant battles with rodents, the spoilers of one's personal efforts to enhance the place. But then I take a walk—slowly, because of age— in the purity of these surroundings, and, sure enough, the rhythm of walking brings back my gladness to be alive. Again there is a cozy feeling and an assurance due to the companionable, enormous, pervasive whole. It takes me back into my right place and into connection with the protective vastness of wilderness, to become a believer again after the slight maladjustments have been walked off. This is why I like my life in Tepitates. Here there is always a resolution of whatever the difficulty is. Discontent evolves, hardly noticed, into contentment. No need to push it; just wait and it happens.

I like living in Tepitates because ninety percent of the time, or maybe ninety-five, I have my wits with me, intact. Although I defer to what by far outsizes me in this untouched environment, I feel on top of my sensibilities. My five senses are also intact. Living naturally as the animals do (not as city folk would call it) keeps me alert. No matter what the surprises or interferences, I can take them in stride. Because I am introverted and accustomed to isolated country, I take life the way a wild thing would: tired, I sleep; playful, I play; hungry, I eat. Like the animal, I am always up to date on my needs and keep close to myself. I can never get too much of this.

Most important is the lack of city din. Instead, there are the quiet and serenity, broken only by equally quieting elemental noises: the whistling of the wind, thunder, cries of animals on the hunt, the caterwauls of the coyotes talking to each other in the distance as part of their hunting—and always, everywhere, the bird sounds. The animal sounds, especially the lone shriek of a puma, are like punctuation marks in a great, silent poem. The sounds come only to help me understand better what they want me to know.

No two days in Tepitates are alike. If the weather stays slightly similar, there will be a happening. There might be a bobcat lazing in the sun on the boulder below, in no hurry to move; a fox might turn up to check the handout bowl; and always, there will be a new bird not seen before. Once I spotted a twinkling glowworm in the evening. Almost always there is a new wild visitor to keep me realizing that the chaparral is filled to the brim with life. If none comes, the lizards are always lying around in the sun. Their eyes are so knowing as they tilt their heads to see me better and do push-ups to make me laugh. I hope the roadrunner will not turn up on his once-a-year visit to harvest them, one by one, choking each one until its body goes limp and then swallowing it whole.

In time, though not often, a brightly marked diamondback rattlesnake will be there before me, his tongue flipping in and out to pick up my scent. If I get too close, he speeds out of sight and into the sagebrush.

Sometimes the deerflies drive me crazy, when there is no breeze to drive them away. I have learned to stay indoors, where window and door screens protect me. Never mind; what I might have done outside today can as easily be done tomorrow. By then, the prevailing north wind will have come around for its routine patrol of the coast and driven the flies away.

Walking quietly and savoring the scene, feeling the cool, gentle air on my arms, becomes sheer pleasure. In the fall, the ever-ready California thrasher sings his conglomeration of tunes. The various migrating species are everywhere. A cottontail rabbit hopping into the brush catches my eye, his white button the last of him to disappear—I read the footprints in the dust, always lost in thought—this is the life. The inner happenings reveal themselves when I reach out to pick up a small, round stone or a stick with bends and twists in it, suggesting something. Or a piece of the outer crust of a boulder, decorated with intricate medallions of moss, shows itself. And always there are the smooth, small, red manzanita limbs. My pockets fill up with small replicas of what catches me from within. The pockets are then emptied; in the house, the treasures look quite decorative after all. Why am I drawn to the shapes and curves and faint colors? I do not know. But I love them. Must we always know?

Walking slowly down the road or along the trail, indulging in these shapes and subtle shades, becomes a kind of merging that makes me feel alive. At the same time the contemplation of death, only a few years off, fits because the year is dying too, as it always does in September. It all makes sense. Merging is one word for dying. And then there is rebirth, nature's rebirth, which may not be mine except in some unexpected way. I do not want to speculate about that. Trusting that whatever happens has meaning, as I trust the meaning in the wilderness, I am glad to follow the year's fall pattern. Merging with something as big as nature, as big as wilderness, gives one comfort. Perhaps there is instinct in these feelings. But even so, to see the year end and feel it end is not only instinct but a leave-taking with eyes open.

The paw tracks on the road this afternoon somehow seem important. In the dust, the record is clear: they are mostly fox tracks—families of them! Big ones, middle-sized ones, and little ones, and here and there the almost dog-sized prints of a coyote. No raccoon today. A clean set of deer tracks threads its way among the others; was the deer looking for water or finding a way out of puma country? Quail have been there too, cutting across the road into the brush. Tiny chipmunk tracks run every which way. Here is the slither trail of a small reptile. Mice, rats, skunks, and all the denizens are there. Scurries here and there could be insects.

And then there is the moonlight. Last night, the moon had been full and the air still; not a thing had moved. My impression had been that everything vegetative was somehow lit, although light was not evident. The fleeting quality of the wild scene had given an impression of lightness—a feeling of light itself, even though it could not be seen.

I like living in Tepitates because the little bit of housekeeping required here touches a nesting instinct that rarely needs to be expressed. In the country, nothing looks as dirty as things look in the city. Also, here, the problem of clothes is reduced to a minimum. Each morning I slip on a bra, a pair of underpants, a blue shirt, and a blue-jean jumper. No thought is needed, only a minimum of effort. Oh yes, a comb through my hair, which has not been cut for three months. Nothing on my face except for fresh water, and then, for going outside, a pair of Top Siders and sometimes socks to match. With these maneuvers reduced to basic simplicity, one's subjective life can flourish.

Subjectivity, because of my many years of living in this wilderness, has gained an increased importance for me and may need more outlet than it would for someone who grew up in civilization. Maybe not. It just might be that all people who are denied quiet because of our frenetic society need this kind of life. When I think about how much time I need for reflection and how difficult and prolonged is the process of resolving conflicts for those who are "civilized," I do not wonder at the insane, superficial, tragic lives everywhere. Hardly anyone in our whole, wide world, except those who were born in the country and know what they are missing, will try to get enough time in nature or enough natural solitude to be human and sane.

I believe it was because of ranch living that I could and did survive boarding school and was free to cut away from my schoolmates for good. Had I hung on to them, I would never have been able to transcend the limited consciousness of the "privileged" few they represented.

Tepitates provides specimens of wild plants for our Kentfield garden. There is a challenge in encouraging them to grow that is deeply satisfying. A tiny green leaf or shoot appearing magically on a cutting put in water or in the earth is like a revelation, almost an epiphany— the appearance of the Other—a life with its own laws. Even though I have cut the shoot off from its parent plant, I never lose the feeling of having to discover its needs. There is also the feeling of being on the side of life and, if the cutting prospers, the feeling of life's being willing to endorse me. This is not a sense of power. It is the feeling of being in tune with life, of going along with life but not being able to influence it in any way. It is being a part of life that also contains death; and soon, if I am lucky, it may mean being essentially no different from the native *Calochortus* proudly upholding its large seedpod, about to shatter and reseed itself.

What bothers me about my life in Tepitates is the shock that takes me totally unaware after my husband and I spend months alone, scarcely seeing another person. When there is a gathering or birthday party, or more than two friends drop in, or there is an occasion to dine in a restaurant with friends, I get hit. I sit like a bump because the conversation is superficial, gossipy, or just joking. Life in Tepitates has been serious, and I have taken it as the norm. Then, in the company of others, life around me becomes light and airy and positive and warm and friendly. I find myself feeling undermined and wanting to break out in unacceptable talk. In an effort to behave, I become tongue-tied, unable to function in any positive way. So much seriousness makes one quite unacceptable to the majority of others, even the nice majority. The shift of attitude comes as a shock. I am left feeling inferior, an extraverted moron or a moronic extravert, and I am. I wonder, then: is there a price for solitude, reflection, consciousness?

Home again in Tepitates, I am grateful for the conducive quiet that allows me time to think my own thoughts. Also, there is time to read other people's published thoughts, which I can put away in my thoughtful storeroom for future use. Occasionally, as I have with Gregory Bateson's unforgettable comment, "Without context, there is no meaning," I adopt the thought in its own words. Then the author's statement is given the chance to take on permanent importance to me. If it sticks, so be it. If not, my own separate experience or an item from the storeroom of thoughts can continue to take precedence. In this way, collective thinking and personal or individual thoughts take their places in my system. This feels like a normal balance. But only in Tepitates can I be sure that this balance exists.

It seems true to say that only in Tepitates do I find what is natural for me. And against this experience of naturalness, I find I can take back into civilization a standard for measuring experience that helps guide my efforts to continue to live normally. Since I am not always successful, I can at least use some simple rules from Tepitates to help me get back on track when distractions derail me. A good sleep; the best part of a day spent alone; a walk where there is minimum traffic; reading the books of others who are also concerned about the wilderness; or writing notes to myself, allowing for the mini-brainwaves that pop up in unexpected places and at odd times: this is how I cope. This approach is definitely individual; others have other ways to keep their sanity. I hope, however, that each time another person makes the effort to stand up to the aberrations of modern life, many more will follow. The more people who insist on avoiding a kind of worldwide craziness, the better.

22

BETWEEN CIVILIZATION AND
THE WILDERNESS

~ LYNDA ~

Coming from the wilderness into civilization was, and still is, terribly hard for me. In the city, one must be self-aware and juggle the multiple and often unrelated variables the day brings. In the wilderness, one must merge into the environment to find the rhythm of belonging, a process that requires the dimming of self-awareness. In both places there is need for decision, action, absorption. But the mode of the city pulls me away from my sense of being all of a piece and makes me live on my outer edges. I feel constantly on the alert in the wilderness too, but I am operating from a deeper base that includes kinesthetic perception. I feel fully engaged, but harmonious within.

My mother questions whether the experience of merger with the infinity of the wilderness is a disadvantage in the ongoing development of one's life. Certainly, unawareness of being merged with nature can be a problem if one wants to enter civilized life and expand conscious development. It is a contradiction in terms to be boundless and merged with the wild and at the same time to try to learn about ideas and explore relationships with others. It is possible to do these sequentially, but not simultaneously. The life of merger is without limit, has no dimensions, and has little power to make things happen. And it is unrelated, as city people define relatedness. As I have said earlier, merger with the wilderness is an experience of the Self in its largest sense. It is a sense of oneness with life in which the individual has little visibility or significance but feels held and sustained by an all-encompassing embrace.

The life of conscious ego development contrasts with this in that it involves self-definition, a determination of personal limits, an exertion of will within these limits, and an awareness of one's being and behavior. Life is lived to its fullest when experienced in both realms, hard as it may be to move back and forth between them.

Until I had to perform on civilization's terms, being merged with the ranch provided a steady state of security and completeness. The ranch, the weather, and the routine guided my life. I thought very little about anything; I flowed along with life in its most physical sense. The ranch provided everything I needed, including tests and challenges and the whole gamut of feeling experiences, from exultation to terror. Although the ranch endured drought, floods, and fire, it never really changed, from before my mother's time to after mine. I was held captive, yet I felt completely free.

The fact that the adults left us to our own devices, demanding almost nothing from us in the way of responsibility, and not relating to us much, meant that we children poured our entire expectation of being parented onto the ranch itself. Our responsibility was to the ocean, the beach, the canyons, and the mountains, and to all the living things we found there. Our favorite activity was "exploring," and there were always new places in which to swim, crawl, jump, and run. Yet we always knew where the center of the ranch was, and we would return to it like homing pigeons.

When, at the age of ten, I began to divide my life between nine months of school and civilization and three months of summer on the ranch, I felt the difference painfully. I think I did not come to conscious realization of myself until late, in mid-adolescence, when the demands of my city peers began to impinge on me. All that seemed to matter to that collective of the 1940s was appearance and knowing the "right way" to behave. Popularity was the goal, a goal I could neither appreciate nor scorn. I was caught in a no-man's-land between yearning for the security of ranch life and wishing I could participate in the life my peers found so entrancing. I had a hard year of depression at that time, a mourning I think of as the result of having lost Eden and not knowing where else to go.

Eventually I did learn, more or less, to make the transition to civilization and to find my way in it. In the process, I found that some of my ranch-bred knowledge was a help, while other parts of my experience made my transition more difficult.

For example, as I have mentioned, my learning to help with cattle roundups was a critical part of my entry into ranch life. Its effect on my attitudes became a disadvantage, however, when I tried to enter city life. On the ranch, when I first started to go on a roundup, I was always far behind. The main gait on a roundup is a fast walk, unlike the galloping of cowboy movies. It is hard, though, to get a wise, old horse to keep up a fast walk, especially when the rider is a novice. It was a matter of pride to learn to keep up, but it took a long time for me to develop courage enough to whack my horse or pony with a stick or the reins. In the first place, I felt terrible about hurting him, and in the second place, I was afraid he would run away. Actually, my child's strength could not really have hurt him; the point was to indicate my determination and authority. Most of the horses we children were allowed to ride were quite aware of our fear and inexperience and took advantage of us. Flailing away ineffectually with our heels and perhaps a stick, we would get them into an unpleasant trot, which soon subsided again into a plodding walk. Occasionally, to my horror, one of the men would come up behind me and give my horse a great cut on the rump with his reins. My horse, completely startled, would leap forward, and I would nearly fall off. For a while, I would get a lively ride, more than I felt secure with, and would be relieved when my horse slowed down again to his usual speed.

Gradually, as my courage built with practice, I found that I could take charge more and more, and thus I found my first experience in exercising authority. How clearly I remember the exhilaration of realizing that this great, thousand-pound animal was collaborating with me and accepting my lead! This phenomenon spread into the rest of my life in a number of ways, including a lifelong preference for being my own boss and a distaste for being told what to do. The development worked well in the wilderness, but of course it brought me a lot of trouble in civilization.

By way of considering the opposite side of the coin, I think of my mother's suggestion that she may have been dwarfed by the wilderness. Discussing with her what she meant by that, I found I agreed with her. Working our way into harmony with the environment meant yielding to it and accepting it. It did little good to fight it. Standing up for oneself was a meaningless concept there.

The psychological term "ego" means just that: "standing up for oneself," as well as developing a point of view, learning to make decisions and judgments, and discovering what one wants and does not want. On the ranch, such concepts were less useful than discovering how things were, and making choices accordingly. We learned to be self-reliant, but that quality was born of knowing how nature worked and accommodating to it.

My tendency to accommodate has brought me trouble in civilization even as I have had difficulty in taking orders. Accommodation is one of the modes of wilderness living that does not work well in urban life, since it may mislead people into taking advantage, intentionally or unintentionally. Confrontation is currently a popular concept in civilization, but it debilitates and bewilders me, even though I can see its value in certain circumstances.

The few times I have appeared as a witness in court, for example—not an uncommon experience for a psychologist—I have become sick afterward. The whole concept of the adversary procedure runs counter to my way of living in the world. I can manage to see my part through, but afterward, my body goes into rebellion and makes me pay for having insulted my relationship to life. I do not take sides easily; I find it is best for me to acknowledge and provide for both sides as much as possible. Winning and losing make sense to me only in terms of hunter and hunted, in the natural order of things. Coyotes eat rabbits; rabbits never eat coyotes. This may not be fair, but it is how it is. Humans defeat other humans, and that is also how it is and has always been, but I can appreciate it only in the service of life and death, as in wartime. Struggles for dominance among coyotes serve a function of pack efficiency. I do not know what function it serves for one human to defeat another human when some mutual accommodation might be possible. I do know that humans are adversarial and that is a common, normal characteristic of the species. But I become sick if I participate in the phenomenon.

My ranch experience ill fitted me for this aspect of my species' behavior. Even as my mother and I learned to accept our horses' assertions of their individuality and were somewhat indulgent of their reluctance while going away from home, I am more comfortable in making room for the preferences of others than in trying to get them to do things my way. I have my preferences, certainly; I just hate to fight for them.

In comparing notes, my mother and I discovered another disjunction from society we have both had to struggle with. Growing up on the ranch, we had developed aspects of ourselves that made us seem masculine to others when we attempted to participate in society. As part of developing what we knew to be self-reliance, we had become proficient in ways our culture used to (and perhaps still does, sometimes) define as masculine. We had taken care of ourselves as best we could, trying never to ask for help, and had developed agility and strength so as to be able to do our jobs on horseback or elsewhere.

I remember measuring myself against the tough barbed wire gates in every fence I rode through. For years I could not budge them, nor could my cousins. We would have to line up along the gate and pull together to loosen the wire looped over the fence post that held the gate in place. Closing the gate was just as hard. Gradually, we all grew strong enough to be able to open the gates alone. It was extremely satisfying to be able to do so. We worked toward being able to lift hay bales and hoist our heavy saddles up onto our horses. We rode bareback until we could saddle our own horses. We wore the same sort of clothes that the men did—jeans and boots—which could withstand the rough conditions of our daily lives. To this day, I am still happiest in that costume.

We developed endurance and the capacity to work hard physically all day long, day after day. We became braver all the time and eventually dared to take the horses anywhere the men did, no matter how steep or brush entangled the terrain. Often our horses would object to being stuck in their bellies by sagebrush when we rode through a particularly choked area, and they would jump or buck. We learned to stay on them and ride on through.

We had to learn to improvise, to see solutions that were not obvious. I remember thinking, "But of course!" when I saw one of the men throw down his jacket to cover some barbed wire on the ground. A horse will walk *through* wire and get cut by it or entangled in it, but it will step *over* a jacket. Another time, I rescued a horse that had fallen with his feet uphill while tied to a tree. He could not get up and was in real trouble. Without thinking about it, I knew I needed to haul on that taut tie rope, pulling the horse's head uphill enough that he could get his underneath front foot downhill from his body. Sure enough, that gave him the leverage he needed to get to his feet.

We learned to be physically ingenious, able to look at a situation and move at once to do what was needed. We found that emergencies released extra strength and knowledge, more than we knew we had. We learned to keep our fatigue and injuries to ourselves. If a calf kicked us in the shin, we tried to refrain from limping. Strength, efficiency, "horse sense," stamina, and independence were the most valued qualities, along with the ability to keep our thoughts and feelings to ourselves.

It was a shock to find that these qualities defined us as "masculine" and unrelated in civilization. Suddenly, my abilities and accomplishments were held against me, as my mother's had been held against her in an earlier time. From feeling mature and competent, we were made to feel unfeminine and undeveloped. I did not realize, until at last we began to talk, that my mother had suffered this problem before me. As an adolescent, I had not understood her efforts to encourage me to wear dresses and makeup and to learn to dance and be charming. I had not minded keeping my thoughts and feelings to myself, but I *had* minded professing false thoughts and feelings just to insinuate myself into a way of life I did not enjoy.

Mercifully, there is a wider view now—at least in some places—of what it means to be a woman, and a recognition that physical development is not limited to men, nor personal charm to women. Now a woman can enjoy the feeling of expansion of strength and courage that wilderness experience can bring. Now the wilderness can bring the sexes together in shared appreciation rather than separate them in false definitions of role. A man may be able to carry a heavier pack, but he needs more food, too. Differences between men and women are real, but in the wilderness they do not have to be divisive.

Because I grew up functioning on the basis of my senses and intuitions about the environment, I had little practice in relating to other human beings, a skill that turned out to be very important to a successful life in the city. To relate to other people, I had to learn to formulate thoughts and express feelings. It was a different world for me. My natural response, based on ranch life, was to back away from such communications. They had been unfamiliar, even disallowed, previously, and as such were unwelcome to me. I know now that I showed little on my face in responding to people, leaving them as chilled and cut off as I had felt when I first arrived on the ranch.

Given my preference for unrelatedness, it might seem surprising that I would choose as my profession the practice of psychology. Yet it was exactly what I needed to activate and develop my capacity to relate. As an analyst, I have heard, seen, and felt the power and purity of personal expression, and gradually I have become able to speak the same language. As a result, I feel stimulated and expanded in ways I would have missed had I avoided psychology.

And yet, verbal and facial expression are still an effort for me. Only when alone, or with an animal, do I relax. Being unrelated is most comfortable and natural to this day. The continuing surprise to me is that I keep returning to the city and psychology.

Wilderness and the city reflect the tension of opposites spoken of in psychology. We seem to have a love-hate relationship with both. Perhaps there is an unconscious wish to settle the tension once and for all, by eliminating one or the other. We abuse our cities as much as we abuse our wilderness. Some of us seek to protect one and neglect or denigrate the other.

My own urge is to resolve the tension of opposites by eliminating the city from my life, along with all its excitement, feeling expression, ideas, and entertainment. My impulse is to immerse myself in the wilderness, to enter into it forever and never come out. I cringe when I hear of forests being killed by acid rain or sawed down for firewood, houses, and pulp. Huge desert developments, built-up lakesides, and cheek-by-jowl houses along the ocean make me ache inside. Off-the-road vehicles shock me as they roar by.

Nonetheless, I have owned a small, smelly motorcycle; my husband and I have made a house out of an old boat yard on the ocean; I love taking long, gas-eating trips in a motor home. And even more bewildering to me is my constant return to the city. No one makes me go there; I am compelled by my human need for my own kind. We are contrary, we humans. We want mutually exclusive things and are impatient with having to settle for letting one thing go while we live its opposite. Yet it is this very tension that prompts insight and originality. And if I were not so utterly torn between my hunger for the wilderness and my relish for the city, I would not be compelled to participate in this effort to understand.

City people become personal in their relationships, knowing others as individuals, because of the close quarters they live in. On the ranch, people were experienced in collective terms. The men would shout at us, "One of you kids open that gate!" or "You kids quit bothering that bull!" or "You kids get out of the way!" We were not even identified as "kids," which would have been a title of a sort. Instead, we were objectified as "you kids," almost one word, and held at arm's length.

We, in turn, identified those who worked on the ranch as "the men" and similarly objectified and distanced them. All adults were "the grown-ups" and were rarely identified as someone's mother or father or by name. And my cousins' parents would group us children as "the men" did: "you kids." Even now, I am startled when I am called by my first name. It scarcely feels like mine.

There was simply no issue about being an individual when I lived on the ranch. Only my grandfather held an individual position; he was differentiated as "the Boss." But he was still not known personally, just as he did not undertake to relate to others as individuals. Hence the mimeographed letter to his daughter, my mother, that began "Dear Son."

When I entered city life, I continued functioning in this collective way. It was literally years before I realized that I was offending others by my way of addressing them in generalities. To this day, it takes conscious attention to remember to hold each person in view while I communicate with him or her. My tendency is to speak or write as to an audience rather than to engage with one particular individual who has particular qualities and attitudes.

I learned this process of personal relatedness of necessity when I began practicing as a psychologist. It was a long time, however, before I realized how central to the work is the intimacy between therapist and client. And when I finally understood that this intimacy was similar to the merger I knew with the wilderness, I realized what it was that made psychology so natural a field of work for me. I appreciate the merged state so much; and the special attraction of my work is that the merger can take place with my own kind, in a way impossible in the wilderness. Therapy and the merger between analysand and therapist (which the therapist should be conscious of, for the security of both parties) is another way for both to reconnect with the lost source of life, the Self.

From this realization, I have come to believe that we have a special need as refugees from the paradise of being unconscious of individuality, our own and others'. We need to be one with something larger than our single selves. We need merger with the whole environment, whether it is experienced through immersion in the wilderness, or intimacy with the process of the psyche as found in the sanctity of the psychologist's consulting room, or in the container for the heart and soul that a church or temple can provide. For some, just knowing that such things exist, or absorbing them from a fine work of art or music or poetry, serves the same purpose. To make art of one's own provides the same benefit. The inspiration to create is a lovely merger with something larger than ourselves.

No sooner do we become aware of our separation from others, realize ourselves as individuals, than we crave to be reunited with something. The great religions are based on this need, and psychology addresses it just as energetically.

But the wilderness was the first source for all of us. It is what we came out of, and it is what draws us back. We have been away from it so long, through our millennia of urban life, that we are only dimly aware of its call. I am sure that for many people the separation has been too long; the call is no longer audible. Religion, philosophy, or art will be a more likely sanctuary for them. But for others of us, especially those of us who have known merger with the wilderness early in life, only the wilderness will provide for our return to the great Self.

23

THE BIG SOMETHING

~ JANE ~

August 1987. These days, I am spending more than I can afford on fees for lawyers who tell us we can preserve the ranch as a wilderness even though it is now divided into hundred-acre lots. Obviously, I hope the lawyers are right. I want to—have to—preserve this special place; I feel that the ranch is not only my birthright but a greatness in itself, something to honor and protect.

Since my sixties I have been asking myself why, even now, this part of the world means so much to me. The answer slowly emerges: it is because this place holds infinite meaning, beyond my understanding. The infinitude of this land is such that I will never get a final, definitive answer about its meaning, unless it comes at the moment of my dying. Nor will anyone, perhaps. The wilderness is an unending stream of life; this is its basic meaning. Beyond that, we cannot know more than our individual limits of articulation allow us.

During the fourteen years of family and personal struggle that followed my father's death, I had the opportunity to experience and enjoy the ranches in my own way. Since then, I have lived six months of the year in this wilderness, in my house in Tepitates. Out on my horse during those fourteen years I came across more natural life than one meets ordinarily, and, paradoxically, I came face to face with the prospect of death, specifically my own. The wilderness explained death dramatically. The horse became death's symbol in my dreams at night and the means by which I found life in all its forms by day.

The series of horses I was privileged to ride while we still owned these lands, combined with the wilderness setting, had much to do with my meeting a long-overdue need to retreat into myself and assimilate the past. This retreat, a kind of psychic descent, was directed by the guidance that wilderness provides if we make ourselves sensitive to its messages.

Life and death, and the overall continuation of life, are what matter. Without death there could be no continuation, for there would be no opportunity for nature to promote new life. "A life for a life" is part of this message, for humans as well as for wildlife. Were I to live forever, how could my descendants get past me and into their own lives? Even if I proved to be the greatest thing on earth, I would still be a physical and psychic deterrent to future life.

The imprinting that happens from the beginning of life sets limits that one can never change, no matter how aware of them one becomes. Imprinting means what it says. In 1908, when I was three, the wilderness was boss. All of us, including my parents, had to knuckle under and abide by its laws. We had no mammoth, destructive machines to back nature off and out of our way. If there were to be changes, *we* had to change, not nature. Although this was, and still is, a privileged experience of nature, we were limited by it.

By having to adjust, all of life, no matter how small or big— including us—becomes part of evolution as nature means it to be. I also like to think that because of that fact, we on the ranch preserved an invaluable and life-giving attitude toward what was greater than each of us. Scientifically minded meddlers had not yet conquered our surroundings. That is happening in a big way now, and it accounts for the money I am spending to save the wilderness aspect of the ranch. But you watch: the manipulators finally will be defeated. I believe that whatever motivates them—ambition, talent, genius; the hunger for power, size, numbers—will finally make them fall by their own weight. Nature will see to that, because nature herself has limits. Limiting is part of the message from the wilderness; failure is an essential ingredient in nature's scheme. Equal-and-different seems to be part of evolution. I believe that it is not possible for one species to command all others; I believe there will be a correction to the present imbalance of species dominance.

My memory of my ranch years as a child and teenager is filled with how often I was faced with what was bigger than me. Climbing trees, jumping my horse across creeks and over boulders, and scaling precipitous trails were routine daily occurrences. My life was constantly at risk. With each threat I had deliberately to put myself into the hands of fate, always knowing there was no guarantee of the outcome. In a way, life on the ranch became a prayer to the elements and the forces that might get me through whatever hazard I was meeting. Each crisis was somehow a blank time, a time out, or a state of nonexistence, a gap in the continuity of ranch life. Each event was a spell of unreality—a jump into the unknown. The situations were so much bigger than I was that without knowing, I developed a habit of placating the vague, unspecified bigness in the situation. That "big something" would, I hoped, somehow protect me.

Because of my having had to adapt to this oversized life, when I moved into civilization, with its many concrete protections, I felt a sense of there being too much of me. I felt conspicuous. My overdeveloped capabilities, especially the overutilized will that had become part of me, were a useless adjunct that got in the way. The expertise that had supported me in physical situations on the ranch became redundant in the city, where I was not threatened in my daily life. (This may not be the case today; now, city life is far more dangerous than life in wilderness. It seems that as wilderness is being destroyed, human instinct is turning ugly.) When I moved from the ranch to the city, I was left floundering, with a sense of inner bigness no longer appropriate.

On the ranch I had unconsciously found, through experience after experience, that there is an Other greater than me out there. Because

I usually came through my adventures unscathed, I concluded that the big something must have been on my side. As a result, I unknowingly cultivated the habit of looking for the missing helpful, monumental Other wherever I was. In the city, the sense of the outer Other would not go away; it left me with a nostalgic yearning for my life among the overpowering elements. The civilized concept of God had never seemed real to me. And the more separated I was from the wilderness lands, the more mythicized they became in my fantasies.

Slowly the equivalent greater-than-me inner Other made itself felt as more constructive. This all-encompassing inner Other finally manifested concretely in a confrontation with the depths of my psyche and in the exploration of psychic phenomena with others who also honored this realm. The autonomous character of this inner phenomenon, especially its self-regulating attribute, eventually linked me to my childhood memories of the overpowering, autonomous elements of nature.

This knowledge of the similarity of the inner phenomenon to the outer experience came to me only in my old age. My yearning for the elements of the past had evidently had a corresponding yearning for the Self, the greater-than-me within.

When I revisited the ranch in my late fifties and early sixties during the six and one-half years of the liquidation process, I thought I was saying good-bye to my childhood lands. But it was during that time, without warning, that I discovered the connections between childhood's experiences and middle age's psychological pursuits. Still later, in old age, came the conscious reconciliations of the outer and inner forces.

In a book about Gnosticism, I discovered that even at the beginning of the Christian era some people had thought that God "resides concealed in nature" rather than being in charge of it. John Muir came to the same conclusion. So, according to some, nature contains God! Some Gnostics were saying that nature is greater than God. This made sense to me; I could accept nature as "out there," with its own laws, while I was "in here," contained by the big something that was sympathetic to nature.

I was not conceptualizing nature as beyond, or over, or above me. Instead, that inner, over-life-sized center had evolved into a certain consciousness. I had been coping for years with natural inner and outer forces beyond me. The consciousness I gained from these efforts finally became a normal part of me that found its outlet in efforts to be original—in other words, to be myself. This usually happens when I am in a natural setting.

Perhaps one could say that this "beyond ego" experience was and is an experience of the archetype of origin, and that its inward-outward manifestation is the source of creativity. I feel sure that this is so, because I nearly always come to life at those times when the inner, self-regulating system connects with the outer reality—when I am in Tepitates with wilderness around me. This is the time when the outer, elemental forces stimulate the inner, and the inner greater-than-me enhances the extraordinary meaningfulness of the outer. It is an experience of completion.

24

THE WILDERNESS AS A HEALING POWER

~ *LYNDA* ~

I believe that the development of consciousness, especially that prompted by the Renaissance, is at least one cause of what I perceive to be the wound of our time, the wound of abandonment. I have wondered, in fact, if one could say that the greater part of the work of Western psychology today has to do with the "psychology of abandonment."

Other wounds resulting from family disturbances, cultural distortions, and social pressures continue to appear, as they always have. But all these injuries of civilization are aggravated by the deep feelings of abandonment, labeled long ago as existential anxiety, that come with self-awareness.

Consciousness—self-awareness—is triggered by fear, pain, grief, and hunger. (Love and other positive experiences are also important for consciousness, of course, but they belong to another discussion.) In our culture we are separated from our mothers at birth, and separation is one key to our development through life. Each generation experiences still earlier separation; nowadays children go to day-care centers and nursery schools before they can walk or talk. I think these children mostly rise to the occasion and cope with their situations, as children have done throughout history. In spite of the casualties, children manage well enough that we have never had to fear for the survival of the species!

Most children growing up in Western cities are not now, and have not been for centuries, held enough, protected enough, or allowed enough time to mature. We become aware of ourselves very early because we are asked to relate to the outer world so early on. There is so much to scare us, to cause us pain, grief, and fear, and there is never enough solace. An array of adults takes care of us, providing good care and not-so-good care. We may have to wait to be fed—and for small children, that is terrifying. All these states of being—hunger, pain, grief, fear—force us to be aware of ourselves and awaken our consciousness.

As soon as we realize ourselves, our initial harmony with the environment is lost. We are thrown out of Eden, and the tension of conflict and frustration grabs us. We begin to notice things, to realize that we have to protect ourselves, and to process what happens to us. If there has been an idyllic merger with a central, protective adult, male or female, it is soon disrupted. Too soon, that adult no longer responds to our needs as soon as they emerge. No longer does that adult provide a safe place for us to nestle in; no longer does he or she predigest life experiences for us, as a wild animal predigests food for its young.

But each bad experience, beginning with separation from our mothers at birth, is also an opportunity to develop new consciousness, new self-awareness, and new techniques to protect our individuality. As each such experience leaves its cut in the flesh of our security, we become more conscious and more sensitive to pain and anxiety. Psychotherapy and other forms of psychic healing have moved into this breach, with their methods of providing a safe place, a re-creation of the original "safe place" with the mother-person (male or female). From this safe place, the client can explore not only the wounds particular to his or her life but also the wound of abandonment that we all share. As we discover the inner security of the Self, the wound of abandonment begins to heal.

~

On the ranch, the train provided one of my early childhood jolts toward consciousness (and toward the "ego," which is part of what we eventually need to go "beyond," for healing's sake). The Southern Pacific Railroad ran its trains the entire length of the coast ranch; in my grandfather's time, this was more than twenty miles of lovely ocean frontage. The track dominated the view to the ocean, with high trestles over the mouths of some of the canyons and cut-and-fill marring the rest of them. I wonder now at my great grandfather's willingness, before the turn of the century, to permit this invasion of his land. As a child I took it for granted, of course, along with everything else about the place. In fact, the train figured in a recurrent dream I had during my years of finding a way to relate to the ranch. I would be running down the track and the train would be roaring up behind me, threatening to run me down. Perhaps the train represented the frightening power the ranch had over me then, an inhuman and merciless power that I could neither face nor escape.

There were times when the train *was* frightening. On foggy summer mornings, we would scurry across the tracks to the beach, goose-pimply over the possibility that the train might emerge suddenly from the fog and be upon us without warning. And sometimes while heading home for lunch, when we were still young enough to have to do that, we would cross the tracks as the 11:20 A.M. Southern Pacific Daylight came south toward Santa Barbara. If there was still fog hanging low over the tracks, the train's headlight bearing down on us would seem huge and ominous, diffused as it was in the fog. It was hard to tell how close the train was on those occasions, so we always assumed the worst and jumped to safety.

Driving big herds of cattle along the beach was easy; the difficulty came with crossing the tracks onto or off the beach. It was a major project to put a thousand or so head of cattle through the gate on one side of the tracks, then contain them over the narrow railroad crossing and through another gate on the other side of the tracks. Tension was always high; no one quite believed the train schedule, so there was constant anxiety that a train might come at any time. Because of the canyons that ran parallel to each other down to the beach, we could not always hear or see the trains at any distance. We were always waiting for a train suddenly to appear around a bend or through the cut the track made through the canyon walls. The cattle responded to our tension by becoming excited and disorganized. Instead of marching docilely across the tracks, they would rush alongside them, east and west. We would hurry after them, our horses slipping and stumbling in the heavy gravel of the rail bed. I never saw a train hit a cow, but I do remember times when we had to split a herd, some on one side of the track and some on the other, because of a train coming. I particularly remember the shouting and tension of the whole process, which may account for the recurrent appearance of the train in my anxiety dreams.

Living with my grandparents was lonely, and I longed for a pet. But Grandmother forbade a dog in the house. My mother and her twin had kept a remarkable collection of wild animals in the basement, but Grandmother's tolerance for that had evaporated by the time I came along. Grandfather's big, yellow dog, Topper, lived outdoors, but since Grandfather was also outdoors all day, every day, Topper was not deprived. They went everywhere together, Topper following Grandfather's horse when he still rode regularly, then riding in the back of the blue Jeep when that replaced the horse. Topper would hang his huge head forward between the seats, drooling all over Grandfather's shoulder and barking at everything. His long, feathered tail swung incessantly from side to side; Topper was as gregarious and talkative as Grandfather was solitary and silent.

My solution for a pet was brief and not very satisfactory. Outside the window of my room was the roof of the screened-in porch below. I was forbidden to go out there because the roof was too weak to hold my weight. But I put a big box of sand out there, where I could reach it by leaning out the window, and installed a horned toad in the sand. My mother says that the horned toads are gone from the ranch now, and I am sorry, because that little beast, a sort of frog-shaped lizard, was very engaging. He seemed armored; his leathery, layered "shell" extended on his sides into little projections, and if you ran your finger along these he would curl to one side in response. I think the important thing for me was the fact that he responded. There was the sense of a personal relationship. Ranch life had so little that was personal; people did not interact much, except in the transaction of some project or activity. To relate just for the sake of relating was rare. So, for me, being with animals more and more replaced relating to people.

My merger with the wilderness, which served as a replacement for human intimacy and healing of the abandonment wound, thus included merger with animals. Even now, when I am in open country or a forest, I am attuned to animals—birds less so, although as I get older I am discovering my connection with them, too. I do need a personal, individual relationship with the wilderness; for me, wildlife provides that link to the impersonal realm of earth, vegetation, and sky.

For years, though, I noticed little about the ranch consciously; my responses were instinctive. A city child would have been far more aware of herself in her surroundings. I absorbed my environment, felt it, took it in through my pores, but I did not see it. My mother describes noticing color on the place only when it was about to be sold. Similarly, the first time I noticed color on the ranch was just before I was to be married. Without thinking about it in words, I knew I had to go to the ranch one last time before that event. Everything would be different after marriage; though, again, I did not articulate the thought, even to myself.

I went for a week's visit during spring vacation from college. A roundup was in progress; the men were collecting cattle from one end of the main ranch and moving them down the beach to the other end. It was March, and the ranch was a violent green. The intensity of color was unpleasant somehow; it made me uncomfortable. My usual sense of the ranch was of dryness, dust, sparse tan grass, and the oppressive sun glaring down. Usually, the only softening factor was the early morning fog—heavy enough, sometimes, in summer that the trees dripped and I had to wear a jacket. It was a good way to start the day; by the time the sun had beaten its way through in late morning, we would have covered a lot of ground and become immersed in our work. It is harder to start up in an already hot sun.

That spring of my last year as a girl, the ranch was showing an aspect of itself I had not taken in consciously as a child, when I was living there year-round. It was a shock to see the greens; even the sagebrush looked green. Seeing the color was a measure to me of how far from the ranch my life had taken me. It was new to be noticing more than the great, geological forms and the quick movements of animals and birds, which my mother had also noticed in her early years on the ranch. I felt loss, and, in retrospect, I think that the old abandonment feelings were activated.

One form that had been an intrinsic part of my merger with the ranch was the great headland I have described as a landmark on the western end of the Bulito's cove. When we looked up from our play on the beach, it was usually toward the massive, black side of the headland; often the sun would have worked its way behind it, so the headland would be shown in profile. I remember only occasionally looking east to the other end of the cove, which was marked with a concrete breakwater. I never asked why the breakwater was there; I suppose it had been built to protect the railroad track on the cliff a hundred feet above it.

The other principal form that impinged on my awareness was the massive ridge that ran along the backbone of the ranch parallel to the ocean. It extended as far as I could see east and west and was a secure boundary to lean against while feeling the infinity of the ocean extending away in front of me—to China, we said. When we would sometimes find a glass float from a fishing net, we wondered if it came from China.

Consciousness of where we are and of the threats to our security, while causing anxiety and a vague sense of having been abandoned, is also essential for survival in city life. Alone in the wilderness we also experience fear and isolation, but we have a history of millions of years of relating to the wilderness literally and bodily. We have a much briefer experience of relating to the world psychologically, with the horrifying anxiety of knowing so much, yet never enough. For most of human history, it was enough to assign power to natural phenomena to appease our anxiety. Entering the wilderness and its microcosms—gardens and parks—gives us an opportunity to reconnect with that instinct and rests our fragile psyches from the exhaustion of trying to stay intact in the civilized world, which is so alien to many of us.

I wonder whether our sometimes cavalier attitude toward wilderness is a result of not knowing the value of finding a way into it, to reconnect for a time to the lost Eden, the Self. It does not address the wound of abandonment to take a dirt bike or snowmobile into the wilderness. Obviously, these machines do provide their riders with satisfaction of some sort, or they would cease to exist. But as I see it, the riding of machines in the wilderness has to do with further development of mastery, control, and power, which are ego qualities. The main reason riders have for going to the desert or to wide-open snow fields appears to be for the space, for room to run the machines. Thus, the true cause of anxiety, the early wound of premature loss of security, is masked by greater and greater strength. The Self that mirrors the wilderness, the whole nature of the individual, is missed, and there is no healing of the wound. There is strengthening of the techniques to endure it, but no healing.

I wonder what city people seek when they visit the country. Do they go to a campground in the forest for a few days in order to set up camp near others and spend their time in connection with other people? Do they take the trip as an opportunity to catch up with the family, struggle up a mountainside, and make as many runs down the ski slopes as daylight and lift lines permit? All of these activities have value, of course, but they are not relevant to healing the wound of the loss of Eden, of abandonment.

Merger with nature is a precious luxury for everyone. And it is dangerous; in the reality of nature, one hunts or is hunted. Never can any creature relax its attention without risk. Yet, for those of us who divide our lives between civilization and wilderness, even a brief experience of the silence that hums while we sit still or move quietly through it will bring us to ourselves, will bring us refreshment and renewed enthusiasm for life. Merger with a therapist can heal our abandonment wound, but merger with nature can reconnect us to the ancient roots of the Self as well.

I think our household animals need this renewal too. My dog used to bloom in the wilderness; she would change her behavior from the city stance of being tall and on her toes, ready to cope with cars, people, and other dogs, to something less domestic. In the wilderness she would move differently, closer to the ground, her tail held low and not waving as it did in the city. Mostly she kept her nose to the ground, again in contrast to her posture in the city, where she would hold her head up to keep a constant watch on all man-made activity. In the forest she led with her nose, but she was clearly alert to all her surroundings. Her heritage as a wild animal could work for her here; she did not have to use her eyes so much. Indeed, her eyes would change; they would become yellower and unrelated to me. Watching her in the wilderness, I found an increased recognition of how the wilderness affected me. She was pursuing business of her own, whereas in the city she mostly pursued my business and so remained closely related to me.

When we came out of the forest, she would be tranquil and content to lie around and sleep. Whatever anxieties and disturbances she had been carrying, as evidenced by restlessness, scratching, or barking, had been washed away by her time in nature. She too had experienced its healing effect. A walk in a city park would not soothe her in the same way. Tension and anxiety would continue as before; the only benefit would have been stretching her legs and getting a bit of air.

For me, then, wilderness has several components. These components are what make up my memory of the ranch: the sense of infinity; the natural elements of dirt, vegetation, and animals; and the cyclical processes of seasons, birth, and death. There is, in that imprint of wilderness, an utter reliability. This reliability is what I have come to know as an inner and outer necessity. My sense of myself at the soul level depends in part on being mirrored back to myself by the terrain and atmosphere of that freedom. It is far more than physical freedom, though it is that, very powerfully, too. I need the sense of fencelessness and openness, the absence of restraint. I need freedom from supervision, observation, and protection too, even though I become anxious as a result. I want to be unremarkable in that terrain, just another part of it. And I do not want to make any changes where I go.

One's choice of wilderness—desert, forest, mountains, or ocean—comes from imprinting, among other things. In the last analysis, the wilderness carries the meaning of home for the soul, at least for those who knew it while growing up, as a particular house means hearth and home for our daily selves.

Limiting ourselves to our homes can be disturbing. By the same token, it might be better not to limit ourselves to the wilderness. There are those who do, and they have something special to say as a result. But they are relatively few.

It is necessary, however, to know a wild area that feels right. For some, a park is just right; for others, it may be a garden. My grandmother's garden was such a place for her. She spent a lot of time in it, her long, light hair twisted up and covered with a red cowboy bandanna. For her, the array of exotic plants and trees, growing untrammeled and in no particular order, apparently gave her a special satisfaction, judging from how much calmer she would be after working there.

The healing for me that comes from being in the wilderness is the opportunity to leave ordinary consciousness and return to my animal, instinctual way of being. Returning from such an experience, I feel restored. I have once again been "taken up," this time by nature, and for a while I am not abandoned; I am found.

I assume that each person discovers his or her own way to relate to the wilderness. But I believe we all share in our need for access to our *idea* of the wilderness in order to keep our souls nourished. What I do not know is how common is the experience of merger with it, or how necessary it is to discover that intimacy when young. Can one come to it as an adult? My mother speaks of "reaching into the mood of the place," "calming" herself, aiming "toward the big letdown I craved," "getting back into my skin," and, finally, "going down to meet the land where it lay." I use all these methods to reenter a merged state with the wilderness, but I need to do it alone. I wonder, too, whether merger would be possible at all had I not discovered it as a child and become conscious of the discovery when I lost the ranch. The ability to merge at will is a joy for me, and it makes me feel safe in the rest of my life. I know that my soul and I can always go home for a rest.

What does frighten me is the prospect of loss of all the wilderness in our world as I have been imprinted to know it: infinity, unmediated seasons, wildlife. Where would my soul go then?

The death of wilderness would be an incomprehensible experience, beyond cycles and the rhythm of birth and death. It would be a sterilization, a one-sidedness as shocking as prison. No attitude could sustain us then; no garden or park could sustain us because the image of the archetype they manifest would have been shattered. The reason a human-made, human-sized phenomenon can work for us is that it is a reference to something greater, something infinite. We may not actually have to be in, or even see, the wilderness for it to reconnect us to the Self, the feeling of completeness. But we do need to know that it exists. Then our local bits and pieces of it in domestic form can keep us linked, as a letter from a dear friend sustains the link of friendship. A garden without a wilderness to refer to would no longer connect us to the infinite. The call to save the wilderness is a call to save us all.

If our wilderness is destroyed, where will we go to recover our relation to our physical and psychic selves? There is nothing else quite like it. Because we emerged from the wilderness, we need to remerge with it to heal our feelings of abandonment.

The phenomenon of consciousness is remarkable; we humans have taken the gifts of adaptability, curiosity, daring, and cognition and built remarkable systems with which to interact with our environment. In order to protect our creativity, we need now to honor the great resource that was our first mother: our wilderness. Attention paid to the wilderness will give us the heart and soul we need to continue our quest for the meaning of our presence in the vast universe.